W9-AGT-463

I've Become My Mother...

I've Become My Mother...

✤

and other observations

Joyce Schenk

Writers Club Press

San Jose New York Lincoln Shanghai

I've Become My Mother...
and other observations

All Rights Reserved © 2002 by Joyce Schenk

No part of this book may be reproduced or transmitted in any form or by any means, graphic, electronic, or mechanical, including photocopying, recording, taping, or by any information storage retrieval system, without the permission in writing from the publisher.

Writers Club Press
an imprint of iUniverse, Inc.

For information address:
iUniverse, Inc.
5220 S. 16th St., Suite 200
Lincoln, NE 68512
www.iuniverse.com

ISBN: 0-595-23356-2

Printed in the United States of America

For George, my constant inspiration. And for Becky, Sherri and Tim, as well as Ryan and Rachel, the next generation.

Contents

I've Become My Mother

I passed a mirror yesterday and suddenly stopped in my tracks. There, wearing my clothes, was my mother, looking back at me.

It was one of those transforming moments in life when reality shines its pure, white light into the brain. I had to face the truth. I've finally become my mother.

There have been ample clues, of course. One of the most pointed came a few years ago when my brother, Alan, a prime supporter of my checkered career in writing, called to remark on my photo in the paper. His comments were the kind of thing a kid sister comes to expect from her big brother. But, though spoken in fun…I think…I had to admit there was truth in his words.

He said, "You know, of course, that picture makes you look like Mom on a bad hair day."

Later, I took time to study the photo objectively. And I had to admit Alan was right.

There was that slight frown, so like Mom's, etched between my brows by long, often futile efforts at understanding what makes this bewildering world go around. And the eyes looking back at me from the photo had many of the same characteristics as my mother's eyes. Even a slight smile makes them squint up. When caught in a full-fledged laugh, the eyes all but disappear into slits, making me look like a happy Asian grandmother. And there are those drooping eyelids, stretched from a lifetime of smiling at the unending comedy of life. Those are definitely her's.

1

The nose and the upturn at the mouth…Alan was right. No wonder he said the photo looked like Mom. And there was no denying the bad-hair day, either.

Of course, the reason for all this similarity lies in the genes, those itty, bitty pieces of what makes us who we are, passed down from mother to daughter to granddaughter and on through the generations.

For instance, in addition to the facial features and the rounded-if-lumpy figure, I've inherited Mom's low cholesterol readings. That's a nice family bonus.

Unfortunately, she also passed along her arthritis-prone joints. Heredity is, after all, a collection of mixed blessings.

But, it's not just in my physical appearance and medical characteristics I've become my mother. Now that I'm being honest, I have to admit that for years I've heard Mom's words coming out of my mouth.

I can remember when the kids were trying to cope with the inevitable stresses and sorrows of their teenage years. As I tried to encourage them, I couldn't seem to stop myself from saying with cherry assurance, "This, too, shall pass."

Vintage Mom.

Apparently, just as I have become my mother, my now-grown daughters are beginning to follow the same generational tradition. Daughter Sherri recently reported a conversation with her husband, Jack. At the end of the discussion, Jack shook his head and said in frustration, "You're beginning to sound just like your mother!"

And so, the genetic transfer continues.

Tastes Can Take Us Home Again

A wonderful sort of magic takes place when our senses are touched by some long-forgotten taste. It's as of that room in our minds where the past is stored away, suddenly opens, and we're transported back to our yesterdays.

I took that memory trip recently when I ordered a piece of coconut cream pie at a home style restaurant.

When I was growing up, this particular kind of pie was one of my mother's specialties. Through the years, I've searched for a duplicate to Mom's unforgettable coconut cream pie. And though I've sampled many pies from other bakers, I've never tasted anything quite like hers.

When the pie I ordered at the restaurant was served, I could only stare at it for a moment. The fluffy mcringue with its sprinkles of coconut decorating the top, was browned ever so lightly. It looked exactly like Mom's delicious coconut cream creation.

Still, I was convinced it couldn't possibly taste the same.

But, when I took that first bite it was like stepping back in time. Suddenly I was sitting at the kitchen table for an after-school milk and pie break. Mom was standing at the sink, wearing her familiar red and white apron. Over everything there was a dusting of flour, evidence of baking day.

In the warm glow of nostalgia, I ate that restaurant piece of pie as slowly as possible. Each creamy bite was pure joy.

For all of us, there are so many memories that are tied up with tastes. Some, like the pie, can magically take us home again. Others may bring back a school picnic or a visit to grandma's house.

Unfortunately, it's getting harder and harder to reproduce the savory flavors we used to love. One reason is that we live in the era of fast foods and boxed mixes.

There's another reason it's so difficult to rediscover those wonderful tastes that live only in our memories. Our mothers and grandmothers cooked everything "from scratch", never bothering to write their recipes down. They knew instinctively how much of this and that went into their special dishes.

For instance, among our all-time family favorites were the huge pots of vegetable beef soup Mom made so often. The thick, rich soup was a genuine meal-in-a-bowl. Into the big soup kettle, Mom threw soup bones, meat, and whatever vegetables she had on hand. The variety was constantly changing, depending on the season. Yet, no matter what was included in the pot, the finished soup always had some special, unidentifiable flavor that I can only attribute to Mom's love.

Through the years, no matter how many different combinations of ingredients I've tried I've never been able to duplicate the taste of Mom's soup.

Not all of the tastes that can take me back to my childhood are tastes from home. In fact, I know that if I would combine a handful of buttered popcorn and a chunk of a Hershey chocolate bar, I could be transported back to the neighborhood movie theater and the excitement of Saturday afternoon matinees.

Today's kids are storing away more memories of Big Macs and pepperoni pizzas than of home made ice cream and fresh-pulled taffy. But no matter what they enjoy most, in time they, too, will find that tastes have the power to bring back the past.

It's been said we can't go home again. But with a little help from our taste buds, we can at least recapture some of the flavor of long ago days.

Money Laundering
Makes Sense

Here we are again, right in the middle of one of those nasty cold and flu seasons. Seems nobody's safe from the curse. Sneezing noses, watery eyes, scratchy throats…they're as common as after-Christmas bills at this time of year.

We all know such maladies spread easily among those working in crowded areas. Every school provides an ideal location for ongoing virus/bacteria exchange. And, even before they reach school age, munchkin-size youngsters carry on the longstanding tradition of passing along the latest illnesses to siblings, parents and grandparents.

But though these close personal contacts are the basis for many of the ailments making the rounds at this time of year, there's an infection transporter that's even more efficient and widespread. I came to that conclusion last week as I stood in the grocery check-out line.

When the lady ahead of me paid the clerk for her purchases, the cute young checker paused, cash in hand. Suddenly, she rocked back, caught in the throes of a mega sneeze. Still sniffing, she pulled a well-used tissue from her pocket and wiped her nose as she rang up the sale. The cashier then gathered the change from the drawer and counted it out to the waiting customer.

There was no doubt in my mind that along with the money, the sweet Typhoid Mary clerk passed on the nasty virus causing her cold.

This scene is repeated thousands of times a day in outlets across the country ranging from large malls to small grocery stores and gas stations.

For decades scientists have been blaming the spread of disease on everything from rats to flies, from fleas to water. But I'm convinced dirty money, passed endlessly from hand to hand, is the major culprit. Of course, ailments like hives, insomnia and arthritis have other causes. Yet for those miserable cold and flu viruses that travel endlessly between strangers, germ-laden money appears the most likely carrier.

There may be a solution ahead for us. Modern technology has been working hard on alternatives to our current forms of money. These innovations might just provide an answer to the problem of germy green-backs and contaminated coins. Credit cards already reduce exposure to money-borne diseases. And, if banking leaders have their way, we'll soon be paying for everything from groceries to gasoline with debit cards.

In the future, we'll probably have a cashless economy. With today's Visa, Master, Discover and dozens of other plastic-card substitutes for money, we're already halfway there. And if there's no actual money in circulation, far fewer cold and flu germs will be passed along from hand to hand.

But the cashless society is still only in the planning stages. Until bills become obsolete, replaced completely by electronic transfers, we'll just have to take up money laundering or live by checkbook and credit card alone.

It's a germy world out there.

In Pursuit of the Perfect Purse

It's an ongoing search. Somewhere out there is the purse of my dreams.

When the subject comes up, my husband, who has watched my handbag hunting efforts for 40 years, simply yawns and says, "You'll never be happy until you find a purse with wheels and file drawers."

He obviously doesn't understand the seriousness of this problem.

After all, the right handbag is vital to a woman's sense of confidence, her feeling that she's in control of at least one small corner of the world.

With this in mind, I've continually searched for that special bag to fit my lifestyle. Along the way, I've gathered a strange collection of not-quit-right purses. Whether made of cloth or straw, vinyl or leather, they each offer different features. Yet they share a common failing. None is large enough to hold all my must have equipment.

The problem, of course, is that I refuse to leave home without taking a good part of home along.

Most women seem to be content to carry a wallet, a hankie, keys and a few touch-up cosmetics. But in addition to these, my basic on-the-road paraphernalia includes pens, a little notebook, sun glasses, reading glasses, a small magazine for those unforseen waiting times, notes on current projects, sales coupons, basic medical supplies ranging from aspirin to Band-Aids, and numerous other essentials that can change with the hour, day or season. In other words, the purse I carry must be less Saks Fifth Avenue, more Samsonite.

When I look back to my early years, I can see my need for the mega-purse came with adulthood. In my teens, a large bag was the last thing

I wanted to carry. Instead, one of those colorful little plastic clutches easily held all my essentials.

And, I can't blame my big-purse obsession on my ancestors. Former generations showed none of this purse preoccupation. I realized that when I was given the little handbag my grandmother took to social events. Made of tiny enameled metal pieces, the small treasure was carried by a loop of fine chain. The wee pouch is smaller than a paperback book. Given the size of the tiny container, I'm sure Grandma limited her away-from-home supplies to little more than one of her exquisite lace-edged hankies.

Fortunately, my daughters have not been afflicted with my purse passion. In fact, daughter Sherri prides herself on being able to squeeze everything she needs into a stylish fold-over bag with a slender shoulder cord. When I watch her unload this amazing holder, I'm certain she has a trap door hidden somewhere in its deepest recesses.

Still, for me only a large size, exceptionally roomy, well-divided bag will do.

Some years ago, I thought I had found the ultimate candidate for my all time perfect purse award. It was a massive leather container with at least five separate pockets. Its heavy over-the shoulder strap was attached to the purse with strong metal rings. The fact that the treasure was blue, not the universally appropriate colors of brown or black, caused only momentary concern. With all its other outstanding features, I quickly decided blue was my new favorite accessory color.

The purse became an indispensable part of my wardrobe…for a few months. Then it began to self-destruct along the seam lines. In the end, only duct tape could have saved my bulgy blue friend.

Since then, my search has gone on. In every store, at each garage sale or flea market, even at social gatherings, I'm continually on the look out for that elusive treasure, the perfect purse.

I'm beginning to think my husband is right about those wheels and file drawers.

The Charm of
Chautauqua in Winter

The jingle of sleigh bells echoed across Chautauqua Institution's snow-covered Bestor Plaza.

I stopped by one of the ancient maples to watch. The sleigh with its cargo of chatting visitors was pulled by a team of strong work horses. The shaggy animals puffed steam into the air as they clopped along on the packed snow. It was a living Currier & Ives image.

The scene was a marked contrast to the Institution's summertime face.

Anyone who has visited Chautauqua during her nine-week summer season knows her as a charming and stimulating Victorian lady. When lectures, classes, and cultural performances fill her days and nights, the air she breathes is charged with excitement.

We discovered Chautauqua during a long-ago summer and instantly become devoted fans.

Like many summertime visitors, we assumed this lovely lady went into hibernation when echoes of the last lecture faded from the Amphitheater and the crowds of visitors left the gates at season's end. But a few years ago, we decided to take an off-season drive through the Institution's grounds.

It was one of those rare days of blue sky and sun above the sparkling white of new-fallen snow. Chautauqua was dressed in her winter best. We realized then that this delightful lady offers more than just a summer love. Like a beautiful and complex woman, she shows an entirely different side of her personality to those who stop by in other seasons.

In spring, she glows with new life.

And after the busy summer season, she finds relaxation by painting herself in the glory of autumn.

Then comes winter.

When the snows blanket the gingerbread cottages and blustery winds whip around the deserted practice studios, when the Athenaeum stands guard above the empty beach and the Miller Bell Tower sends its voice along ice-covered streets, Chautauqua is a mature woman of quiet beauty.

Since we discovered Chautauqua's wintertime personality, we visit her often during her soft, silvery months of peaceful contemplation.

The tranquility doesn't mean that the lady's asleep. Far from it. Though Chautauqua's winter setting is deceptively quiet, in reality much goes on across the grounds.

The bookstore, a regular stop on the rounds of most folks visiting the Institution any time of year, continues throughout the winter to be a center of activities. Seven days a week the staff dispenses everything from newspapers and books to artists' supplies and candy.

It's here the hardy outdoor types rent their cross country skis and the less adventurous buy tickets for the traditional Chautauqua sleigh rides.

I have a special reason for making frequent bookstore stops in the winter. Since there are fewer folks browsing than in the busy months, I can take my time to sample each book that catches my interest.

The Smith Memorial Library, too, maintains winter hours. It's always a haven for those who want to warm both body and mind.

In her winter-wonderland period, lady Chautauqua moves to a slower, quieter pace. And that pace is captured by the movement of a horse-drawn sleigh as it glides through this Victorian fairyland to the accompaniment of bells, jingling in the frosty air.

When "Uh-Oh" is the Only Answer

Most questions in life can be answered with "yes," "no," or some informational phrase that fill the needs of the questioner. But, there are times in life when a question can only be responded to with the surprise or dismay of a simple "uh-oh."

As an example, I remember the time when, early in our marriage, we were visiting George's family in Pennsylvania from our home in Texas. We were browsing in a store, when a delivery man came in and said, loudly, "Who owns that Texas car outside…" Before he could finish, we smiled and said it was ours. We were sure this was the beginning of a warm welcome to the Keystone State. You know the kind… "I lived in Texas for three years and…" Instead, the driver continued, "because I just backed my truck into it."

Uh-oh!

In another car-related incident, I recall several years ago we were in the final stages of preparation for our snowbird trip from New York to Florida. The car was packed. The engine was running. We were saying our last seasonal good-byes to neighbors. As we closed the car doors and buckled in, one friend stopped waving and pointed to the the front of the car. "Hey," he called out, "how come there's a puddle forming under there?"

Uh-oh!

Another question that struck a feeling of dread in my heart was one my son, Tim, asked innocently on a warm afternoon as we worked together in the kitchen. He reached into the freezer for a package of frozen vegetables. With his hand deep in the innards of this important storage space, he turned to me and said, "Why is everything in here so soft and warm?"

Uh-oh!

Then there was another busy, kitchen centered day when Tim stooped to get something out of the cabinet under the sink. He turned to me with a dripping container in his hand and asked, "Why do you suppose there's water all over everything under here?"

Uh-oh.

One errand filled day, I made supper preparations early by putting together a meal in my favorite kitchen helper, my Crock Pot. Once the meat, potatoes and carrots were arranged in the pot, I turned on the switch and gathered my things for my marathon shopping and stopping jaunt. Half-way through the day, I called home to see how all was going and check in with Tim.

After assuring me all was well, he finished by saying, "I was just wondering, Mom, didn't you want this Crock Pot plugged in?"

Uh-oh

But my worst uh-oh experiences came one afternoon when I was deep into an important writing assignment. George was busy with a do-it-yourself project. And, with both of us working at opposite ends of the house, we were not paying the slightest attention to each other. Suddenly, near the end of the long piece I had worked on for hours, the computer screen went blank. I sat in shock for a moment before I heard George's voice calling from the distance. "I just turned off some of the power. It didn't affect your computer, did it?"

Uh-Oh!

Maple Sugarin' Time
Means Spring

Spring's coming!

No, I haven't seen a crocus yet. And the first welcome robin hasn't arrived to search our yard for worms. But the earliest sign of spring is evident throughout the area: the sap buckets are hanging on the maple trees.

When Mother Nature begins her first tentative stirrings, the folks who produce maple syrup are quick to put their taps in place. For me, the sight of a towering maple with buckets on her hips is the surest sign that the age-old clock of the seasons is turning toward spring.

On a bright, warming winter day, you can stand beside a tapped tree and listen to the sweet sap trickle into the buckets. It's the sound of the reawakening of life.

I'm always amazed at the energy and dedication of those who catch, collect and convert the maple sap to syrup. After every sap-rising day, they make the rounds of their tapped trees, pouring off the liquid and rehanging the buckets. Some of these tireless folks tap as many as 1,000 maples.

In dozens of little out-of-the-way sugarin' houses, the fires burn continuously for days, as the syrup makers tend their evaporators.

Depending on the sweetness of the sap, it can take as many as 60 gallons to make just one gallon of the dark, delicious syrup. And, what a tremendous amount of work is required to get that gallon from the tree to the table.

I recently read that some enterprising folks in New England have come up with a new way to add to their annual maple syrup income. For a fee…something in the neighborhood of $25…anyone can "buy" a maple tree. For the investment, the "tree buyer" is guaranteed at least a quart of maple syrup, supposedly from his own tree.

To someone living in San Diego or Houston or Orlando, the idea must sound pretty appealing. It would certainly provide for some interesting breakfast table conversation, especially when house guests are present.

But, those of us who live right here in the middle of maple syrup country are fortunate. We don't have to go to such lengths to get our supply of the luscious syrup, fresh from the maple. It's only a short time from the sight of the first sap bucket to the morning when we can enjoy the sweet taste of a successful harvest with our breakfast.

Bring on the pancakes. I'm ready to welcome spring!

Bits and Pieces of Useless Information

There was a time when my mind often hosted a flash of understanding or a semi-creative thought. But lately I've found the frequency of these episodes has decreased. In fact, I'm beginning to realize something strange has taken over my thinking processes, especially my memory.

I think I have "trivia-itis!"

For instance, I have instant recall for such vital information as the state flower of Texas (Blue bonnet, of course), but I still have to look up the phone numbers of some of my best friends.

And, when my husband asks "where is last year's income tax file?", I draw a blank. Yet I can tell you word for word the lyrics of the songs from "Carrousel."

I recently filled out a form that required me to enter the license number of the car. I couldn't for the life of me remember it. But, as I took a peek out the door to read the plate, I overheard someone on the radio asking, "Who wrote *The Fountainhead*?" My trivia-filled mind immediately supplied the name Ayn Rand.

In discussing this strange phenomenon with friends, I've been comforted by the fact that I'm not the only one afflicted with trivia-itis. There seems to be a lot of the malady going around.

I don't want to admit these cases are simply the inroads of age on the brilliant minds of my generation. Instead, I've been looking for other causes for the problem.

One of these, I'm sure, is the country's current love affair with trivia.

The growing collection of game shows on television is making the bits and pieces of random information stored throughout a lifetime seem a valuable resource. Though the big budget newcomers to the TV line-up are drawing a large and enthusiastic viewer ship, the grand-daddy of them all, "Jeopardy," goes on its quiet way as a family entertainment staple.

Each evening, our little trio watches Alex Trebek challenge three sweaty-palmed contestants to search their memories for some of the most insignificant information they have ever come across. Like thousands of other "Jeopardy" fans, we join the fun by pitting our wits against the show's big board of clues.

My score, if it were recorded, would usually be pretty dismal. Yet I'm constantly amazed at the broad range of trivia the show's participants have stored away.

Maybe the stimulation of the television quiz shows is having an affect on me, but I'm finding my recall of trivial trifles is growing with each year. Unfortunately, the really vital information of life…like the calorie content of a small Dairy Queen cone…is slipping away.

All I can hope is that I will eventually get so good at this trivia thing that I, too, will be judged worthy of a place as a contestant on "Jeopardy!"

But, knowing my fickle brain, just about the time Alex wants the question to match, "This popular singer was known as 'Old Blue Eyes' and 'The Chairman of the Board'," my mind will immediately be filled with such facts as my friends' phone numbers, the location of last year's income tax files and the calorie content of that small Dairy Queen cone.

The Natural Need for Naps

Science has finally confirmed what you and I have known all along: the human body was meant to have an afternoon nap.

According to some recent findings, researchers are now saying naps could help people to maintain alertness and improve mood. Scientists report "there is a strong biological readiness to fall asleep during the mid-afternoon, even in people who have had a full night's sleep".

I didn't need anyone to tell me that. The tendency I have to nod off after lunch has convinced me my alertness definitely takes a break at that time.

The afternoon nap was a part of my growing-up years in Texas. It goes with the lifestyle in many areas located near the equator. Folks who live in the southwest have long been influenced by their Mexican neighbors' tradition of "siesta". In fact, when I worked in Texas in the usually-hectic setting of a large hospital, I found the pace of work always slowed down between one and three in the afternoon.

That certainly suits my own daily clock. Without a nap, my afternoons become a time for prolonged yawns and drooping eyelids.

When our kids were tiny, their afternoon nap time of 2:00 was a great opportunity for me to doze a little and recharge my batteries for the early evening demands of motherhood.

Some folks believe mid-afternoon sleepiness results from eating a large lunch.

On the contrary, researchers have found that a dip in alertness occurs whether or not people even eat lunch. In an article I read on the subject, Roger Broughton, a professor of neurology at the University of

Ottawa, said the sleepiness depends solely on the time of day, not on eating patterns.

Dr. Broughton went on to say that in a research project, the volunteers, on average, began their naps about 12 hours after the middle of the main period of sleep. That means someone who sleeps from midnight to 7:00 AM, would be ready for a nap around 3:30 PM.

Dr. Broughton concluded his findings with, "This study gave us the first conclusive evidence that the afternoon nap is internally generated by the brain as part of the biological clock for sleep/wake cycles".

So those of us who are nappers finally have the understanding and blessing of science when we curl up on the couch or stretch out in bed and "catch a few Zs" in the afternoon. After all their research, the "experts" have concluded it's perfectly natural.

But you and I knew that all along, didn't we?

Excuse me, I'm starting to yawn. It's time for a you-know-what.

Mothers are the Family's Martyrs

An informal survey of my friends has convinced me every family has one or more members in the throes of the current hacking, honking, hankie-holding epidemic. Colds and flu are definitely making the rounds.

One pal has played host to the same nasty virus for weeks, and the dratted little critter shows no signs of leaving her for a more robust host. She recently groaned in a raspy voice, "I sound like Harry Belafonte on a bad day."

From past experience, I can tell you that if you're going to come down with this traveling misery, the sooner you can get it, the better. By the time the rest of the family and most of your friends have been through it, it's become and old, tired topic. There's no sympathy left for those who are last in the infection line.

While the late comers are wheezing away in relative obscurity, the fortunate who have already recovered have moved on to more timely complaints. The world seems to have no interest in providing a soothing, "Oh, you poor thing!" to the still sneezing members of the Kleenex society.

Generally, the folks at the bottom of the community illness barrel are the mothers.

That's because these pillars of the household are convinced they can't allow themselves to get sick until the rest of the family has recovered. They feel it's their job to lay in a good supply of juice, load up on a selection of cold pills and cough medicines and gather together the materials for their most effective home remedies. Mothers throw all their experience into getting hubby and children back on their feet again.

Then, and only then, can mothers finally admit to feeling punk. And, with the rest of the family once again basking in the glow of good health, mom finally allows herself to go to bed.

But, by this time the medicine chest holds only one cold pill and the cough medicine is down to a scant teaspoon. The juice supply, of course, is only a memory.

So the stricken mother of the house suffers in martyred silence. But, if she can muster the effort to use her theatric ability, at least the family will eventually recognize what a selfless sufferer she is.

I can remember my Mom dragging herself out of bed in the midst of a three-day migraine to get my sack lunch ready for school. It was a sad sight. Watching her made me feel she was some kind of saint, a mother far too good for the likes of me. After one of these heroic efforts on Mom's part, I was totally humbled. I cleaned up my act and willingly pitched in washing dishes, making beds and doing my own lunch…for at least a couple of weeks until the spell wore off.

I suspect the headaches only lasted for one day. But Mom used the second and third days of the siege as a learning experience for the rest of the family.

I've tried Mom's training technique on my family, but I apparently don't have the theatrical talent to really sell it.

However, I do remember one time that the family united to pamper me. I was a 28-year-old mother who had just nursed three kids through the misery of the mumps. When all was finally back to normal, I suddenly found myself stricken with this kids' disease, a very un-funny experience for an adult. This time I was really sick. Fever, sore throat, body aches…it all made me feel absolutely awful.

The family pitched in and took wonderful care of me. But I was a bit perplexed when each loved one who came into the bedroom stifled a smile and left my bedside trying not to chuckle. I thought they were taking this situation with far less seriousness than it deserved.

That was until I managed to stagger to the bathroom. There, looking back at me from the mirror, was the biggest chipmunk face I'd ever seen. To make the sight even sillier, the huge cheeks on the pale face were glowing a feverish shade of bright red. No wonder my family had a hard time facing me without laughing. It was not my finest hour.

But today's crop of colds and flu are far less serious. Although annoying and frustrating, the maladies don't pose a long-term threat to the well-being of the victims. Since the stricken ones know the viruses will eventually fade away, they can take heart as they sniffle their way through each day. There's bound to be a light at the end of the tissue-lined tunnel.

I Have a Need to Knead

I've learned to accept the fact that I'll never make it into the Martha Stewart Homemaker's Hall of Fame.

As a cook I serve the family a well-balanced, but not spectacular, menu of nutritious food. There are no blue-ribbon masterpieces, no unforgettable gourmet surprises. It's a basic, down-to-earth kind of fare.

But in one area, I've achieved consistent triumph that overshadows any other domestic shortcomings. I'm a bread baker.

When a friend dropped by recently and saw the fresh-baked loaves on the kitchen table, she said enthusiastically, "Oh, I see you have one of those new bread makers, too."

I laughed and told her, "No. A bread making machine will never have a place in my kitchen!"

You see, I simply have to get my hands into the bread dough. I have an inborn need to knead.

There's something basic and satisfying about mixing all those simple, old fashioned ingredients…eggs, butter, flour, salt, sugar, yeast…and creating fragrant loaves of bread.

For me, the best step in the process is the act of kneading that soft, resilient dough. It gives me a deep sense of connection with past generations.

I began baking bread when the kids were small. By the time they started school, I often sent them off with homemade bread sandwiches that never failed to get comments from classmates at the lunch table.

After the kids graduated, I slowed down on bread baking for a while. After all, there were now only three of us and my standard output of four loaves often overwhelmed the available freezer space.

But recently, I've put the bread-making apron back on. Since few of our neighbors bake, I've found a new and appreciative audience for my bread. Now I give away two loaves, put one in the freezer and immediately slice the heel from the remaining loaf. (Long ago I claimed the steaming heal as the cook's reward.)

Through the years, I've learned there is a mystique about homemade bread that seems tied in with security and motherhood. In fact, I once heard a top-notch real estate salesman advise homeowners, "When you get ready to show the house to potential buyers, try to have some bread baking in the oven. The smell alone will make them feel they've found their new home."

The perfume of homemade bread is almost as potent as the taste!

If I had one piece of cooking advice for new brides, it would be to learn to make homemade bread...from scratch. The very act is a labor of love. And few offerings are more welcome at the family table than a steaming, fresh-from-the-oven loaf of this staple of life.

You may want to try the recipe I've used for more years than I care to remember. Here it is, with my love:

Delicious White Bread

In a large bowl, mix:

> 3 cups hot water
> 2 Tablespoons butter or margarine
> ½ Cup sugar
> 2 Tablespoons salt

When the mixture is lukewarm, stir in:

> 2 eggs
> 2 packages dry yeast

Add in:

> 9 to 10 cups white flour. (I mix in the flour until the dough will accept no more.) After the dough is thoroughly mixed, place it in large, buttered bowl and set aside in a warm, draft-free spot to rise.

Let rise to double in bulk.

Turn out on a floured surface and knead well. Let rise to double again.

Knead once more, then divide into 4 portions and place in buttered bread pans. Let rise to double a third time.

Bake in 400 degree oven for 20 minutes or until bread sounds hollow when tapped.

Brush with melted butter.

Once you get the hang of bread baking, you, too, may find you have been overtaken by that age-old need to knead.

Once a Collector,
Always a Collector

"You amaze me," my mother said. "Give you two bent nails and you'll start a collection."

She was standing in the middle of my cluttered room, known by the family as "Collection Central."

I had to admit, Mom was right. At age 12, I was a hopeless collector. My room was home to boxes of playing cards, albums of postage stamps, cartons of matchbook covers, shelves of Teddy bears and bags of marbles.

And a new fire was beginning to burn in my collector's heart of hearts. My aunts had recently sent me a few picture post cards from their travels. I was hooked.

As the years passed, my delight in collecting never disappeared, even though the objects of my searches changed.

The postage stamps were stored away. The bags of marbles, match book covers and playing cards were passed on to younger friends. Some of the Teddy bears even found new homes. But collections were always a part of my life.

There was something satisfying in gathering interesting items, categorizing them and putting them on display. And when the search was on for a special addition to a collection, nothing quite matched the fun of the find.

Years after my marbles and playing card days, I met a wonderful guy who was an enthusiastic coin collector. It seemed only natural to merge our collections and our lives.

After marriage, our joint collecting interests eventually led us to antique clocks. For several years we gathered these fascinating time pieces. But we finally realized that when a dozen wind-up, chiming clocks mark the witching hour of midnight, the din can disturb the soundest sleeper. Clocks made for a much noisier collection than either coins or stamps.

Antique pump organs were our next fascination. We found these elderly instruments in barns, parlors of old farm houses and even small apartments in retirement homes. Each of the organs needed a loving investment of time and attention to be returned to its original beauty and tone. At one time we had two dozen of these delightful pieces in our crowded house. Every one of the organs finally found a new home.

And it was fortunate the organs moved on, because as our collection of three children grew to adulthood they, too, followed the family instincts to gather and sort. Through the years, the accumulations in the kids' rooms went from stuffed animals, paper dolls and toy cars to record albums, books, and my son's ever growing hat collection. Now all but our son have gone on to their own collection filled homes.

But time has never diminished my own love of collecting. It's simply been modified. For instance, in my office I still have a well loved family of half-a-dozen Teddy bears. These little stuffed friends are much smaller and less bedraggled than the companions that shared my bedroom when I was 12. But they are just as important to me as those I had so long ago.

Now in my grandmother years, I've found I'm no longer interested in gathering growing numbers of items I find interesting. Instead I'm much more satisfied with a single lovely piece…one basket hung on the wall to admire rather than dozens scattered around the house, one fat little china bluebird perched on the shelf rather than a ceramic flock of twenty gathering dust on the what not. Time has altered my collecting instincts to focus on tiny treasures.

But the thrill is still there. At yard sales, auctions and rummage sales I still find myself searching for that special jewel that seems to whisper "take me home".

And, although two bent nails no longer fire my interest to search for more, I've recently developed a fascination with shells. At last count, I'm up to three jars of these beach-combing mementoes.

It's hard to go cold turkey when it comes to collecting.

What's in a Name?

Although we come into the world with nothing, we quickly receive a gift that will go with us throughout life.

It's our name.

But society has a way of by-passing this lifetime tag and designating each of us according to our relationships with others.

For instance, before I entered school, I'm told I was usually referred to as "Joe and Florences' youngest." And, to the kids in the neighborhood, I was simply the sister of one of my siblings.

In school, of course, our names are used to separate us from the crowd. And it's here many folks gain those interesting nicknames that can last far past childhood. Sonny, Cissy, Junior, Peanut…fine for a second grader but tough to shake if you want to become a supreme court justice or run for the senate.

In young adult life, we come into our own. For a period of time we're recognized as individuals with identities separate from the family. Our names go on our business cards, even on our car license plates.

But, once marriage enters the picture, things can again change, especially for women. In my case I became Mrs. Schenk or George's wife. In a few years, I progressed to Becky, Sherri or Tim's mom.

As families develop, children get caught up in another facet of the ongoing name game.

For instance, in the Schenk family, when all went well, the kids were affectionately called Beck or Beckyl, Sher or Sherz and Tim or Timbo. But, if any of the three stepped out of line, they could immediately tell the level of their transgression by the name we used to get their attention. Becky Lynn! Sherril Sue! Timothy Alan!

I, on the other hand, quickly learned to interpret what the kids were trying to get past me by the way they addressed me.

"Mom, where is my blue sweater?" Strictly a plea for information from the family keeper of the clothes.

"Mommy, I REALLY need a new pair of jeans." This always meant the kid was trying munchkin psychology by calling on the first loving name he or she had used for me.

"MOTHER, I can't believe you want me to wear this tacky dress to the party!" When they invoked the "mother" thing, I knew desperation had set in. But, in these cases I remembered my own teen-age years. When I tried the same technique on my mom, she was never swayed by my indignation. And, when it was my turn with my teen-agers, neither was I.

These days, each of the kids is an adult in his or her own right. They are no longer "George and Joyces'" little ones. But, as luck would have it, I now have a whole new group of folks who identify me as a parent of one of these grown-up youngsters.

I'm often spotted by someone who comes up to me with a smile and says, "I thought I recognized you. You're Tim's mom!"

The Losing Game
is Hard to Win

On any given day, a large (pardon the pun) percentage of the population is on a diet.

As a veteran of many battles in the diet wars, I've come away with some sobering truths about this endless struggle to slim down and tone up to meet the standards of my doctor as well as those of a fickle society.

I realize the doctor, at least, has my best interest at heart. As I sit on his examining table, struggling to hold his skimpy gown around my less-than-skimpy body, he points out such benefits of a sound weight-loss plan as lower blood pressure, greater flexibility and a general sense of well-being.

Society, on the other hand, tells me I must concentrate on such things as self image, general attractiveness and the ability to wear horizontal stripes.

Sadly, the same society that makes the stylishly-slim figure the norm, also offers far too many temptations for those struggling to fit in with the slender crowd.

For instance, there's something subversive about the folks who put a motivational fitness/weight-loss article in a woman's magazine on pages 65 and 66, then fill page 67 with an irresistible photo and recipe spread on brownies.

And the fast-food industry isn't much help, either. How many people stop in at Dunkin' Donuts and order only a cup of coffee? Or who makes a visit to their local Dairy Queen for a diet soda? Of course, we all know that the food at McDonald's, Burger King and other drop-in dining places is less than ideal nutritional fare for dieters.

The food industry has tried in recent years to cater to those of us of…let's say "fuller figures." But, if you've ever tried one of the new adaptations of former favorites now labeled low fat, low calorie, you know they have one characteristic in common. When they took out the fat and calories, they also took out the taste.

There are abundant tips for losing weight, many of them couched in humor. I love to read these, since they help me to find some reason to smile while visiting the Womens' Size clothing department.

One of my favorite pieces of advice says, "To lose weight, get a case of the flu, and visit Egypt."

Of course, that great philosopher, Miss Piggy, sticks by her personal guideline: "Never eat more than you can lift."

Still, humor aside, those of us waging the diet wars continue to focus on the newest version of the food pyramid. We try to avoid fats and concentrate on vegetables, fruits, grains and healthy proteins. In fact, I think it's safe to say most of us have collected dozens of clippings of recipes featuring things that are "good for us." Yet, it's hard to give up such favorites as pork chops, ice cream and, of course, chocolate. Well, that last one is on my impossible-to-do-without list. But I have cut back.

I'm trying, along with all my "stocky" friends, to devise ways to stick with a nutritional plan that will, eventually, result in a new me. In fact, I was recently lamenting with a friend about how hard it is to incorporate as many servings of fruits and vegetables in my daily intake as the experts say we should have.

She nodded, then said, "Well, I decided I've definitely been eating too little in the fruit category. But, I solved the problem temporarily. I went right out and had a banana split."

How Wash Day Has Changed!

When I take the time to count my blessings, I always include my automatic washer. If that sounds silly, just stop and consider how far we washer ladies have come.

I clearly recall those long ago days when, as a kid, I helped Mom with the Monday-morning ritual known to every household as Wash Day. From early morning till late afternoon, the focus of activity was the labor-intensive task of turning piles of dirty laundry into usable shirts and skirts, towels and tablecloths.

Monday was not my favorite day of the week. Of course, Tuesday was Ironing Day, but that's another story.

Back to Monday. The wash day set up alone was daunting. Mom, my big sister and I would gather mountains of soiled clothing and household linens. We carried our loads down the narrow basement stairs and dumped the mess on the cellar floor for sorting. Since I was the youngest member of the family washing trio, it was my job to divide the laundry into piles: whites, colored items, towels and so on.

As I tossed scruffy slacks and stained shirts, musty bath towels and dirty sox here and there, Mom and Sis set about arranging the rinse tubs around the asthmatic old wringer washer. Hot water went into the tubs, with a measured dose of bluing for the one designated for whites. Then load after load, the laundry and soap were added to the hot water in the waiting washer. As the wheezy machine churned away, it became a frothy, steaming cauldron.

When the washer had completed its portion of the work, we washer ladies took turns using the smooth, bleached laundry stick to snag out pieces of clothing and start them on their way through the hungry wringer. Today's automatic washer users have missed the thrill of coaxing a determined wringer to give up a twisted wad of bra straps, apron strings and sox, or a rag rug wound tightly around the rollers by its tattered fringe.

And, for the inattentive, this step in the washing process could be a dangerous job. The wringer operator quickly gained a deep respect for the device's inescapable finger-mashing capabilities.

Today, as I do the laundry in our quiet, efficient automatic washer, I still think back to those long wash days. What a blessing it is to turn on our modern genie and walk away, knowing it will do the work for me. When I return, most of the water is spun out of the load and I can simply transfer the pile into the other wash day treasure, the automatic dryer.

The wash tub, the bluing, the dank cellar with its narrow steps, the malevolent wringer……all now exist only in my memory.

No wonder I count the automatic washer among my blessings. Talk about women's liberation, on wash days alone, we've come a long way.

A Pencil Without an
Eraser is Incomplete

As you and I mosey down this dusty road of life together, there are some important mileposts we should notice.

One of these is coming up, and all of us pencil users should pause in tribute. It was on March 30, 1858, that a patent was issued for the pencil with an attached eraser.

As a longtime lover of the pencil, I can't imagine writing with one of these handy and unassuming communicating tools without having to resort, at least once, to flipping it over and using the little nub of rubber on the top.

What did pencil wielding writers do before that little error eradicator made pencil pushing user-friendly? Were folks back then so sure of themselves they never had to make a correction? Or did they simply throw away their writing goofs and start over? I think of the pencil's eraser as the earliest version of my computer's "delete" key. For us mistake makers, nothing beats the ability to rub out our errors, whether we do it with thousands of dollars in electronic circuitry or manually, with the simple little eraser.

I gives me a feeling of sisterhood with that innovative soul who, back in the mid-1800s in a far different world, understood that those who goof during the process of writing needed a way to redeem their works. Just a rub to delete the mistake, then a brush of the hand to remove the error dust, and we can move ahead to a masterpiece.

Through the years, my pencils have come in all shapes and sizes. I've had novelty ones, as big around as my thumb, made for laughs rather than writing. Then there's my favorite slim silver pencil, partner to a matching pen. Along the way, I've also picked up dozens of pencils in various colors, advertising everything from banks to book stores, from hospitals to hotels.

My first pencils, and the ones I still use most, were the familiar orange-yellow Number 2s. From the chubby fists of block-printing youngsters to the aging hands of the country's most beloved poets, these unassuming pencils have served all ages…and all writing forms…for generations. These, like all of my well used pencils, have always come with attached erasers, thanks to the inventiveness of that long ago entrepreneur.

I'll admit that a few of the stubby little eraser-less pencils have crossed my path. The folks setting up golf courses, bowling alleys and bridge tables seem to find these useful. Evidently golfers, bowlers and bridge players limit their mistakes to their games, leaving their score entries error free.

But for my purposes, pencils with no built-in means of correction are useless.

Like that long ago inventor, when I take up a pencil I need the security of an on-board error-eradicator. A well-sharpened pencil, topped with a fresh eraser, is still the most portable of all communication tools.

I'm Nuts About Pecans

My love affair with pecans began during my Texas childhood.

Our next-door neighbors' back yard was home to three towering paper-shell pecan trees. Two of the three spread their branches over the fence, obligingly scattering their annual nut crop throughout our yard.

Mom, the family baker, assigned my sister and I the job of gathering these small treasures and preparing them for kitchen duty. An old hand at nut harvesting, Mom taught us the trick of gently cracking the smooth brown shells in the middle so the meats would slide out in perfect halves. We spent many hours chatting, cracking and sorting the pecans. And, I must admit, we munched our share throughout the process.

There was something unforgettable about the taste of those fresh from the tree pecans. I've never found an equal to it since those long ago days. Yet even nuts that have been on the shelf a while, if they're kept in a tightly closed container, are delicious.

It's been many, many years since my pecan gathering sessions. And these tasty nuts still remain my favorites.

Peanuts, walnuts, Brazil nuts, cashews...all are flavorful treats, but nothing can quite match the magnificent pecan.

Each year when we travel to Punta Gorda, and again on our return trip to Chautauqua County, I make sure to stop at a particular roadside souvenir and fruit stand on Rt. 301 in north central Florida.

In addition to such Sunshine State favorites as fresh oranges, grapefruit, boiled peanuts and bananas, the silver-haired lady who runs the stand maintains a good supply of shelled pecans kept fresh in heavy zippered plastic bags. I buy several pounds to last for the months ahead.

Just opening one of these packets sets my mouth watering. And I can't resist taking a few out of the bag to savor as we drive.

Trying to describe the taste of pecans is like trying to paint a word picture of the aroma of fresh coffee. It's a personal response.

For me, pecans are a staple of the baker's craft. From cookies and cakes to muffins and pies, pecans can turn a ho-hum item into a halle-lujah. Of course, when you combine pecans with my other favorite, chocolate, well, it's simply out of this world.

In fact, they say the streets of heaven are paved with gold. But I'm betting glory land has at least one subdivision where the avenues are done in chocolate and pecans.

Sort of gives you something to look forward to!

No Talent With Tresses

The time has come to admit it. I'm hair-impaired.

It's not that my built-in head covering is inferior. The quality and quantity seem to be about average. And it does all the things hair is designed to do…keep my head warm in the winter and get into my eyes in the summer.

My problem is simply that I have absolutely no talent with the stuff.

Don't think this is just a case of false modesty. I'm the first to say that I do an acceptable job when creating crafts, baking chocolate chip cookies or sewing curtains. But my hair and I have never been on friendly terms.

One example is the disaster that greets me when I first look into the bathroom mirror in the morning. Fortunately, there are no small children around. The sight could scar them for life. It's as though my head and Mr. Pillow had an all-night battle and Mr. Pillow won.

In the cold light of morning even Phyllis Diller's mop looks better than mine. I often get the feeling that nothing short of a whip and a chair will tame the mess. Fortunately, it tends to settle down after some determined work with a wet comb.

This hair handicap has been with me all my life. I well remember my teen years when I'd join my girlfriends for one of those marathon giggle sessions known as a slumber party. One of the rituals observed at these events was the "pin-curl period." It was that dreaded hour or so devoted to rolling your hair in carefully-constructed curls and securing the rolls in place with bobby pins (remember those?). I was always intimidated by my pals whose heads soon sported smooth rolls of hair arranged in such neat rows they had the precision of a military formation.

In contrast, my pin-curls were haphazard lumps that made my head look like an abandoned hay field.

It was embarrassing enough at the slumber party. But the next day at school, when my friends showed off hairdos of shiny waves or bouncy curls, my head was covered with uneven ridges and bumps, like some carelessly discarded shag rug.

As I grew older, I tried valiantly to keep up with the current hair styles, but my success rate was dismal. I flopped with the flip and my bouffant backfired.

When our children came along, I finally gave up on the longer styles. I happily changed to the short hair adopted by busy new mothers.

Yet, even with my abbreviated mane, there were problems. I often sported bent bangs, fly-away necklines and wild tufts that wouldn't stay tucked behind my ears.

Things finally changed when I discovered pure magic at the hands of compassionate and talented professionals. On the day I first dragged myself into a beauty shop, I'm certain I must have represented the challenge of the hairdressers' careers. But they rose to the occasion and set to work with experience and determination. After an intense transformation period, I emerged from the suds and sprays with a halo of well-arranged hair. It was a miracle.

Although the first morning glimpse in the mirror is still a sobering experience, these days my major hair problems seem to be under control. In fact, I'm looking surprisingly human in spite of my lifelong hair impairment. It's all due to my periodic visits to the professional hair fixer-uppers. Time and again, these wizards have managed to bring my head back from the brink of disaster to a state of well-groomed grace.

Even though I still have no talent with my tresses, the pros in the beauty business have finally put me and my hair on friendly terms.

Acronyms: Today's Spoken Shorthand

It all seemed to start out with the word "yuppie," the handy reference to young upwardly mobile professionals. Since then, the American fascination with these handy shorthand references has blossomed into a whole new language.

I recently checked out the internet on the subject of acronyms and found hundreds of listings. There were whole banks of these made-up words, separated into categories. From Public Broadcasting to Plumbing, from Medical to Military, every field of interest, every segment of society now has its own collection of shorthand phrases.

Of course, we've known of the government's love of non-words for a long time. FBI, CIA, IRS…the collection is enough to make any official document look like gibberish.

But, it's not these "official" acronyms I find interesting. Instead, I keep an eye out for the made-up words referring to groups of people.

I decided long ago that I fit one of these categories. I'm a FRUMP, a Frugal, Responsible, Unpretentious Mature Person.

But the latest crop of acronyms seems to include something for everyone from seniors to kids.

A new list features SKIPPIES: School Kids with Income, Purchasing Power. And you may even know some FLYERS: Fun Loving Youth en Route to Success.

You might find you're a member of the MAAFIES: Middle Aged Affluent Folks.

Or, you could be a MOSSIE. A Middle Aged, Over stressed Semiaffluent Suburbanite.

A large segment of today's society is considered DINKs: Double Income, No Kids.

But, many families find themselves in the DIMP group. That's Dual Income, Money Problems.

Large cities like San Francisco have their share of GUPPIES—Gay Upwardly Mobile Professionals.

Then there is the group known to hold views contrary to many of their neighbors. These are the CAVE people…Citizens Against Virtually Everything.

And, many fall into the group of individuals that my Atlanta friend, Tom, claims is his. He once told me, "I'm a WOFFIE. That stands for Well-Off Older Folks."

So, if you ever find yourself feeling left out, with no special group of your own to identify with, take heart. Somewhere out there, there's an acronym that fits your interests and lifestyle.

In fact, you might feel comfortable in the circle I've been thinking of forming. It will simply be known as FAT. No, no, not the overweight kind. This one stands for Fans of Alex Trebek.

Wanna join?

Giving Voice to the Wind

Some years ago, I saw a lovely wind chime in a gift shop. My husband, George, was browsing nearby so I called him over to see this treasure made up of silver tubes and a weighted ringer. I touched the chime and said, "Listen to the sound. Isn't it wonderful?"

Unimpressed with such garden-style enhancements, his comments were limited to a brief "Um-hum."

Yet, when Christmas arrived, his gift was the wind-chime I had so admired. But, wait. It wasn't really the one I had seen. Instead, when I examined the chime more closely, I realized this was one of those wonderful George-made items my handy guy had carefully crafted himself. When I asked about it, he admitted he had gone back to the store and taken measurements of the chime I had shown him. Then he came home and duplicated it.

I was thrilled. Such a gift, hand-made by the most important person in my life, is far more dear to me than one bought from a store.

I took my time finding the perfect spot for the wind chime.

First, I tried it in a corner of our patio. The site was under an extension of the roof where it would be protected from the rains. But the chime seldom sounded. I thought there might be some flaw in it's construction keeping it from ringing, yet when I touched it, the chime sounded loud and clear.

So I decided to move it to a tree branch where it would still be protected from the worst weather, but the breezes would touch it more easily. Sure enough, I began to hear the chime's voice from time to time. Yet my special gift was still silent more often than I had hoped.

Finally, in desperation, I hung it at the edge of a large awning where it would get the brunt of the winds and rain. In this location even the slightest breeze would set the chime to singing. And, on a really windy days, it would have the chance to perform with abandon.

The final move proved to be the perfect answer to placement for the wind chime. Now, each day I enjoy listening to its song as a background to my activities.

I realize now that by trying to protect my wind chime from the elements, I was keeping this treasure from fulfilling its mission of bringing joyful sound to its surroundings, giving voice to the wind.

I guess I'm a lot like that wind chime. When day after day I keep myself safe from the winds and rains of life, I sometimes find myself thinking, "Is this all there is?"

But, like the wind chime, I come alive when I take on new challenges, face up to the changing winds of life. For me and my chime, turning the winds that swirl around us into music is a worthwhile reward for leaving a protected setting.

I've Been Wondering...

In the know-it-all years of my youth, I thought I had all the answers. Eventually, I learned smug ignorance is a frequent condition of the young.

As I've grown older, I've given up any pretense at wisdom. Instead, I just keep finding more un-answered questions about this increasingly-perplexing world of ours.

For example, when bread is exposed to the air, it becomes dry and hard. But when crackers are left out, they get soft and mushy. Why is that?

Why do people drive three blocks to go to the gym for a workout?

How can anyone who stays at a $300-per-night hotel be called a "guest?"

Why do swimmers always run for cover at the first drops of a passing shower?

How is it that some people bring joy wherever they go and others bring joy WHENEVER they go?

When someone inside the bathroom says, "Just a minute", why does that minute seem so much longer when you're waiting on the outside?

Why IS the grass always greener on the other side of the fence.

Why don't "wise guy" and "wise man" mean the same thing?

And how can it be that, even though I used the same ingredients, my home made soup has never tasted as good as my Mom's?

Here's another one that has always made me wonder. When I look in the mirror, what's left becomes right and what's right becomes left. How is it that what's up doesn't become down?

Another thing that puzzles me involves the migration of geese. Just how does the flock choose the goose to fly at the head of the "V?" Is it a democratic election or is the eldest given the honor? Or is the flock simply led by the one who has demonstrated he knows the best way to the destination?

And why is everyone from book publishers to map-makers using far smaller print these days than they did when I was a kid?

Since the bills on the baseball caps are designed to keep the sun out of the wearer's eyes, why do so many guys insist on wearing the caps backwards?

What is it about fishing that can draw otherwise sane individuals out in the broiling sun to sit for hours in an expensive boat and drown shrimp or worms in an effort to catch a slippery critter the pole-holder has no intention of keeping?

Why is it the foods advertised as fat free and sugar free are also taste free?

And why do the womens' magazines insist on printing a luscious-looking photo and recipe for double-fudge brownies across the page from an article on sure-fire diet tricks?

Why are there fifty candidates for Miss America but only two major choices for president of the United States?

These are just a few of the things that baffle me. And the older I get, the more I add to my list. But, from what my friends tell me, I'm not alone out here in "wonder" land. Growing numbers of us are finding the world a constant source of mystery and mirth.

A Gentle Entry into Spring Cleaning

The chores involved in regular housekeeping have never been among my favorite activities. But the simple ongoing rituals of cleaning pale in comparison to the efforts required as winter rounds the curve of the year toward summer. That's when the civilized world declares, "It's Spring Cleaning time!"

For me, those words conjure up childhood memories, undoubtedly colored by time and imagination. As I recall, each spring I scrubbed miles of woodwork, spent exhausting hours beneath the clothesline whacking dusty rugs with a wicked-looking rug beater and worked on hands and knees removing countless black marks from the hardwood floors. In our house, spring cleaning was a dreaded marathon of fun-less activities.

That dread has carried over into my adult life. When I know the time has come for the annual spring assault on the grit and grime left by winter, I delay the inevitable as long as possible. But the ritual can only be put off so long before the family begins to make pointed comments like, "Gee, it's been weeks since I've actually seen the top of that table."

Yet, even with all the nudging, I can't make myself jump into the spring cleaning whirlpool too quickly. Like a timid swimmer testing the waters, I have to dip in a toe before I can commit the whole foot. So I take on a small chore as a sort of spring cleaning warm-up. This year, I started with my purse.

Laugh if you want, but cleaning out my purse is no easy task. It takes patience, determination and a commitment to rid myself of mementoes of the past. Mine, you see, is no tiny envelope of a bag.

No, this purse came from Australia and, like that country's kangaroo population, it relies heavily on its pouches and pockets to fulfill its role in life.

Separating necessary equipment from the stuff that's no longer essential is a challenge for the lifelong collector in me.

But, on a recent afternoon I finally mustered up the courage to tackle the purse-cleaning project. Though it took more than an hour, in the end I was able to make order out of chaos. I took out a spare pen or two along with a couple of extra little notebooks I keep for jotting reminders. And, with the wastebasket standing by, I discarded a small collection of old notes and lists, an empty envelope, some wadded-up Kleenex and a few aging cough drops.

As I rummage through, I discovered a tiny stash of treasures in one of the deep pockets. There, in the dark reaches, lay a dime, a nickel and two pennies. The coins were obviously the fall-out from some long-ago shopping trip.

With the refuse out of the way, such vital equipment as sun glasses, pen and notebook, billfold, check book, car keys and cosmetics were rearranged to be more accessible.

When I was satisfied I had completed my purse-cleaning project, I carefully replaced the change in the bottom of one of the dark pockets. That way, no matter what else happens in my life, I know I'll always have something to fall back on.

And now that the purse has been restored to order, I'm ready to take the next step on this spring cleaning journey. But I don't want to move too quickly.

I think tomorrow I'll tackle the kitchen junk drawer.

Bubbles Hold a Drop of Magic

There's a special kind of enchantment in those glistening spheres called bubbles. Something about blowing them and watching as they drift away in a breeze seems to capture the kid in all of us.

Do you recall those little bubble pipes we had as youngsters? The colorful bubble-blowers were made up of a mouth tube attached to the pipe's "bowl"—a cluster of small saucer-shaped segments designed to form bubbles.

On a lazy day, we would gather up our bubble pipes and a dish of soapy water, mixed up by an accommodating mom, and go out into the yard to make magic.

A dip of the bubble pipe into the sudsy solution, a long, slow blow on the mouth piece, and suddenly we'd be surrounded by a flock of glistening, dancing spheres. All sizes of bubbles would pour from our pipes, each carrying on its side a miniature rainbow of colors.

I remembered those long ago days as I walked through a toy department recently. There, on a prominent display shelf was a colorful assortment of bottles containing "Mr. Bubbles." I realized that the toy industry was filling the void, since there aren't as many moms at home these days to mix up soapy water.

And, somehow, before I knew it, I had loaded six of the smaller bottles into my shopping cart. Something deep inside told me I'd find a good use for these throwbacks to childhood.

It was only a few days later that I made arrangements to visit my friend, Eloise. It's been a difficult year for this sweet lady. It wasn't long ago she became a widow when her husband of more than 50 years passed away. And, she had just returned home from the hospital after a bout with pneumonia. Eloise, was having a hard time rediscovering reasons to smile.

When I got to her house, I found her resting in her big chair in the corner of her porch. I gave her a hug and said, "The kid in me has come to visit the kid in you."

She looked confused until I took out the bottle of Mr. Bubbles, opened it and used the "Magic Wand" to make a string of bubbles above Eloise's head. Her smile told me that her inner kid was still there and ready for the visit. We talked, laughed and blew bubbles for a long time. Before I left, I placed the bubble bottle next to my friend with strict instructions to open it and make some magic whenever her thoughts were getting gloomy. Her smile as we hugged told me the "bubble therapy" had worked.

A few days later, I stopped in to see another pal, Darlene. A string of health problems has put a damper on the activities Darlene and her husband usually share.

I opened the bottle of kid-friendly bubble mix and demonstrated for the two of them. In a short time, we were filling their porch with bubbles and laughter. We exchanged stories of childhood experiences with those universal bubble pipes. It was a trip back to kidsville for all of us. I gave them the bottle of mix with instructions to continue using the bubble magic when the fun-factor in their lives seemed lacking.

I still have four bottles left from the six-pack I impulsively bought that day in the toy department. I intend to keep one so the little girl that dwells inside me can take a short trip back to childhood when my life needs the boost. But those last three bottles are ready to be shared with other former kids. Do you know anyone who needs a magic-bubble fix?

A Sweet Addiction

There are differing opinions on what makes the world go'round. Romantics tell us it's love. Tycoons say it's money. Those who work in the halls of congress try to make us believe it's power politics.

I can't agree with any of them. You see, through the years I've discovered what really makes the world go around. It's CHOCOLATE!

I know I'm not alone in this carefully thought-out opinion. We chocoholics have known the truth for generations.

A little chocolate in the right place at the right time can work wonders. How else do you account for the success of our GIs in gaining the trust of the people in war-torn countries? U.S. soldiers giving out chocolate candy bars were accepted as heros wherever they went. Forget weapons, the most powerful country in the world is the one with the most Hershey bars…with or without the almonds.

For many chocoholics, Hershey is the standard by which all other chocolates are judged.

Although I have been a chocoholic since childhood, it wasn't till I actually visited the mecca of chocolate, Hershey, PA, that I learned how powerful this addiction to the candy can be.

I was in town to attend a conference at Hershey Medical Center, the OTHER famous landmark in Hershey. My hotel was located in the center of the city. With a little time to kill, I made the mistake of going out for an evening walk.

There was a sweet, lingering fragrance in the air. It was hauntingly familiar, yet I couldn't quite place it. Then it came to me. It was chocolate! The whole town was perfumed with the essence of chocolate!

I filled my lungs with huge gulps of air, trying to breathe it all in. I almost hyper-ventilated on the delicious air.

Suddenly I noticed something that made me stop in my tracks. Atop each lamp post on the main street, there were huge Hershey kisses. The giant-size decorations were hypnotizing.

Half of the light posts were topped with massive un-wrapped chocolate kisses, looking every bit as tempting as their miniature counterparts. And on the alternating posts were huge kisses still wrapped in shiny foil, complete with the little Hershey pull-tab. Although the mock chocolates were only meant to serve as an appropriate decoration, reminding visitors of the city's most famous business, they looked so real I simply stood and stared.

When I was finally able to get my feet moving, I turned and raced back to the hotel. There I locked myself in the safety of my room. I couldn't take the chance of embarrassing my family with a front-page picture in the Hershey, PA, newspaper showing a middle-aged woman desperately climbing a lamp post in a vain attempt to steal a huge bite of the mega-candy treasures on the top.

Since that fateful day of resisted temptation, my travels have brought me other chocolate-centered experiences. For instance, some years ago my brother, Alan, treated me to dinner in a fine restaurant. When the meal was finished, the waiter presented us with the dessert list. There, jumping from the sheet was the challenge I simply couldn't pass up. It was called "Death by Chocolate."

For a moment, I thought of how my family would miss me if I were taken from them while indulging my addiction. Was it worth taking the chance?

Of course it was!

I told the waiter, "If I die, I die. Bring it on!"

When the plate was set before me, I took a moment to revel in this delicacy, a true chocolate-lover's dream come true. The creamy chocolate pie was set in a rich chocolate crust and topped with a luscious chocolate sauce. I savored every bite.

Obviously, I didn't die. But I may have to go back some day to see if it's possible to overdose on such a treat. Those of us who are experienced chocoholics owe it to the public to keep tabs on this type of threat.

It's a dangerous job, but…well, you know.

The Family Rocker is Still on Duty

Although I've had a life-long love affair with rockers, my all time favorite was the sturdy oak chair with the broad seat that George and I bought while we were awaiting the arrival of our first child, Becky.

We found the rocker on the porch of an elderly lady who was selling her household goods to move into a small apartment. As she showed us the chair, she ran her hands lovingly over the curved arms.

A bulging six months pregnant, I awkwardly took a seat in the rocker to try it out. It was a perfect fit. As we paid for the chair, we explained it would have a place of honor in our new nursery. The woman's face creased into a smile and she patted the rocker's arm one last time as if saying good-bye to an old friend.

In the weeks before Becky's arrival, we painted the chair a soft, dove grey and added a comfortable new cushion.

Through the years the old rocker served as a favorite end-of-the-day place for each of the kids. Whether George or I were singing to Becky, reading to Sherri or rocking Tim, we logged many hours in the family's special chair.

Years later the children, now grown into young adults, told us a strange and contrived tale of wanting to "borrow" the chair to show to a friend. When the aging rocker came back home, the worn grey paint was gone. As a surprise, our trio of grown kids had given the family chair a make over. It had been stripped down to its lovely honey colored oak and was once again sporting a new cushion.

Eventually, our family down sized from five to three and we moved into a smaller home. That's when we decided it was time to pass the chair along to the next generation.

Today that old family favorite has a new place of honor in the home of our grown-up first-born, Becky. It has traveled to Australia and back with Becky, her husband Randy and their son and daughter, Ryan and Rachel.

Each has spent hours of enjoyment in this family treasure. It has been the setting for bedtime stories, nursery songs, quiet conversations between parent and child and an occasional naptime.

Today, once again the curved arms and broad, cushioned seat invite family members to slow down and rest.

Each time we stop in for a visit, I have a warm and comfortable reunion with the old oak chair.

As I sit for a moment in its wide, inviting seat, I find my mind drifting back to the nights I held a feverish baby as a young mother. Then, there were those special cuddling times when I rocked Rachel or Ryan and read again such favorites as Goodnight Moon and Home for a Bunny.

It makes me smile to think that the old family rocker is still doing duty as a comfort center for my loved ones.

Small Town Life Holds
Special Appeal

In a recent survey, folks in some of the country's fast-paced metropolitan areas were asked where they would like to live, if they had the choice of any place. Two-thirds said it would be in a small town.

It's easy to understand the choice. In a world that often seems out of control, where reports from the big cities routinely focus on all manner of madness and mayhem, there's something solid, dependable and enduring about small town life.

Here in our little corner of the globe, we have a rich vein of such communities.

Although we can't quite duplicate the simplicity enjoyed by Opie, Andy and Aunt Bea in that fictional village of Mayberry, there are many parallels between that beloved town and the places we in western Chautauqua County call home.

We still have such nostalgic summertime activities as concerts in the park, swims in the lake and fireworks on the Fourth of July. And there always seems to be time to chat with friends and neighbors along the streets and in the stores.

It's a lifestyle that invites people to slow down and get in touch with themselves, their families and their community.

But city folks, even though they yearn for this simpler life, often find it difficult to adjust to the pace we small town residents enjoy.

For example, I remember one Memorial Day in Findley Lake when I was among the spectators lining Main Street as the annual parade marched by. In addition to dozens of local folks, the small crowd included a few out of town visitors. Beside me stood a businessman from Cleveland.

The parade was led by a handful of area veterans, wearing uniforms recently retrieved from attic trunks. The flag bearer proudly carried the Stars and Stripes, as the former service men stepped smartly along the street.

Next came contingents of the local Girl Scouts and Boy Scouts, dressed in freshly-pressed uniforms. Then there were some local farmers, each wearing their best Western-style clothing and riding a favorite horse. There was also a colorful float from a local day-care center, featuring a giggling collection of waving tots.

And, at the end of the line rolled the fire department's shiny red engine, blowing its siren in celebration.

After the brief show passed by and the scattered applause of the village residents faded away, the Cleveland visitor turned to me and asked in surprise, "Is that it?"

"Yes," I said enthusiastically, "and wasn't that a neat way to mark the day!"

He rolled a world-weary eye and said, "I never saw anything so under-whelming!"

But, as I recall, he was back to join the hometown crowd for the next Memorial Day parade.

Through the years, I've come to realize that the rural towns and villages dotting our region's map have many common characteristics. For instance, a small town is where families know each other…the moms, the dads, the youngsters, even the dogs. It's where kids can stop at any house and ask for a drink of water or the use of the phone and not be turned away.

A small town is where a fire department chicken barbecue always becomes an informal reunion of old friends.

In a small town, a house fire or a farm accident brings out not only the volunteer fire department, but the entire community. Quickly and quietly, a caring network goes into action, offering the priceless kind of neighbor-to-neighbor help seldom seen in the big city.

Our area's small towns, like thousands of others across the country, have much in common with one another. Yet each has its own flavor. Each is unique.

And each of our little towns and villages, like the Mayberry of Andy, Opie and Aunt Bea, is a piece of grass roots America where tradition is honored and the sense of community is still thriving.

For those of us fortunate enough to live in these slow-paced, kinder and gentler placcs, thc "undcr-whclming" lifestyle suits us just fine.

A New Barbie for the New Century

Barbie, that ever young beauty from the toy shelf, has at last reached maturity. In fact, Barbie now has more than 40 tiny candles on her fat-free, low-cal cake.

But even as age has advanced on Barbie's perfect figure, there have been no sags, no wrinkles to show the progress of the years. She's obviously the envy of all us seasoned beauties who have no toy company to help us halt the march of time.

Recently, however, in an effort to bring their popular doll up to date, Mattel announced Barbie has undergone some changes. The plan, according to the publicity, has been to give her a "more athletic, natural physique." In addition to wider hips and a smaller bust, Barbie at last has a tiny belly button to replace that unsightly joint marking her middle for so long.

Mattel says the new look was designed to make Barbie "hipper and more relevant" to the girls of today.

I, for one, am delighted to see that Barbie has become slightly less perfect. Flawlessness and reality simply aren't compatible.

While Mattel brings their forty-something doll into the new century, I'd like to propose a number of additional ideas to help Barbie more accurately reflect today's world.

How about a Mid-Life Barbie? She would come with tiny bifocals, sensible shoes and a small bottle of hair color. And, to complete the picture, she would have a shelf of self-help books and a collection of dietary supplements.

Then there could be a CEO Barbie. This lady would be cast in the executive mode, complete with a determined expression and a wardrobe of power suits. The modern, career-oriented doll would carry a notebook computer and a leather-bound day planner. An available companion doll would be a handsome and efficient male secretary. His name, of course, would be Ken.

And, in order to represent a vast segment of today's society, Mattel could offer a Retirement Barbie. She would be dressed in a polyester pant suit, have short greying hair, and carry her own AARP card. Part of the additional equipment for this happy, active doll would be a miniature Florida condo, complete with photos of the grandkids. She would come with a bag of Bingo supplies and a selection of large-brimmed hats to ward off the sun. There could also be such added pieces to this lifestyle as a tiny set of luggage and a ever ready tour bus.

Another winning update on their popular doll could make Mattel a top seller this summer, at lease here in Chautauqua County. It would be Chautauqua Barbie. In this case, the tanned, athletic charmer would be dressed in colorful shorts and top, ride a bike and have stylish sun glasses perched atop her head. The doll would wear a small, laminated pass hanging on a wee cord around her neck. And in her pocket, Chautauqua Barbie would carry a handy Master Card.

That's one doll the folks around here would be happy to see arriving in June.

Chautauqua Institution is Waking From Her Slumber

"The trams are beginning to run," said my friend, Bev, recently.

Like many of us, Bev, who for years has operated the treasure-filled Copper Corner at Chautauqua, has watched this annual reawakening of the Institution with enthusiasm.

Lately, Chautauqua has been undergoing its seasonal transition from quiet hamlet to world-class center for arts, religion, education and entertainment. Each year, during the final weeks of May and the opening weeks of June, this Victorian village stretches and shakes off the effects of the long winter.

In these final pre-season days, the Institution still belongs to us, her residents and her neighbors. It's the perfect time for a last, leisurely drive along the narrow streets or a random stroll down the inviting walkways. Last week, I took time out for just such a visit.

All across the Institution's grounds, sounds of activity filled the air. The voices of saws, hammers and lawnmowers joined in a bustling chorus.

The scene at Bestor Plaza was one of energetic rebirth. In the book store, shelves, racks and showcases were filled with the kinds of books, magazines and keepsakes Chautauquans love.

Windows of the Copper Corner, Viking Trader and other shops along the first floor of the Colonnade were decorated with unique items to draw shoppers.

At the other end of the plaza, Smith Library was in full swing. Since Smith is open year around, the coming of summer simply extends its hours. And now, as the season nears, many incoming Chautauquans rediscover the attractions of this outstanding library.

After exploring the Bestor Plaza scene, I took a slow drive around the grounds.

Some of the houses still sported their wintertime canvas porch covers. But many of the homes were being readied for summer. Workers and homeowners were scrubbing porches, raking lawns, cleaning outdoor lights, planting shrubs and hanging flower-filled baskets.

Activities were also underway at the Children's School and Arts Quadrangle, preparing these important facilities for the coming crowds.

At Bellinger Hall, the Institution's year-around conference center, a few cars were parked in the lot, testifying to the continued use of this popular complex.

Down by the lake, Chautauqua's Grand Dame, the majestic Athenaeum Hotel, was bustling. Workers were cleaning the broad porches, polishing windows and arranging the dozens of inviting wicker chairs that serve as the hotel's traditional outdoor furnishings. Before the season opens, the Athenaeum will once again display the regal glow she has carried for generations.

Before I left the grounds, I drove over to the small park by the Miller Bell Tower. The tower, long a symbol of Chautauqua, seemed ageless. Framed by ancient maples, the brick structure stood against a background of sunlit lake waters.

In this quiet place, on this lovely day, it was easy to imagine what Chautauqua was like so long ago. Founded in the 1870s, the Institution was designed to serve as a summer encampment for Sunday school teachers. It was a quiet retreat for intellectual pursuit and religious instruction.

Today, the Institution is world famous, not just in the fields of religion and education, but in the arts and entertainment, as well.

In late June, Chautauqua will open for another in its unbroken series of over 125 seasons. Then, the world will flock to its gates.

Crowds will visit the tree-lined grounds where Thomas Edison spent his summers, where presidents have spoken, great musicians continue to perform and where actors and authors, world leaders and explorers still rub elbows with the common man.

Though people travel from across the country and around the world to come here, for us, Chautauqua's neighbors, this world-class jewel is "just down the road a piece." It's a unique treasure right here in our own backyard.

The Twinkle of a Sumer Night

Last night I saw something that took me back to my childhood.

Fireflies, like tiny stars sent down from the night sky, danced across the lawn and twinkled their mysterious light. For a fleeting moment, I was a kid again.

I could feel once more the exhilaration of running barefoot through the damp night grass, an open jar clutched in my hands, trying to catch the little dots of living light we called lightning bugs.

Each summer, word would pass among the neighborhood kids that somewhere there was an eccentric tycoon eager to buy collections of the glowing insects. As spring evenings warmed into summer, my buddies and I spent hours planning how we'd make our fortune capturing fireflies.

"Bet I'll get a hundred dollars for mine," David bragged. Martha, never outdone, said, "I'll get a thousand for mine."

Being a few months older than the other two, I felt it my duty to top them. With an air of authority, I said, "I'm gonna get a zillion dollars cause I'm gonna catch more than anybody!"

Actually, in spite of my big plans, I don't remember a summer when I captured more than three or four of the twinkling insects. And I never had the heart to keep even those. They looked so forlorn there in my jar, their light dimming.

So, I'd sneak away from my pals, and in an out-of-the-way clump of bushes, I'd unscrew the jar lid and shake my prisoners back into the night. So much for my dreamed-of fortune.

As the years went by and childhood was left far behind, fireflies continued to hold a special place on my list of a favorite summertime sights.

On a sun-drenched day, I'm easily dazzled by the greens and blues, the reds and yellows that nature so lavishly uses to paint the daytime world. But at night, when all is still, when the colors have given way to velvet blackness and even the wind has gone to sleep, the fireflies come out to dance. Their tiny lights are a welcome sight for day-weary eyes. The fireflies' twinkle combines with that of the distant stars to rule the summer world after dark.

I know that scientists explain the little insects with down-to-earth logic. They tell us that there's nothing magical about these common bugs. Nature has simply outfitted them with a luminescence that attracts the opposite sex and helps to keep the species alive.

There's ample proof of the scientific explanation. The fireflies' glow has apparently been irresistible among the hes and shes of the firefly world, keeping the bugs producing more mini-lights down through the centuries.

My everyday, rational mind knows all this. But it's my whimsical, nighttime mind that thinks of fireflies as a kind of magic.

Their glow can dot the dark with a shifting network of pin point lights. It can come and go without warning. It's a wondrous sight, totally independent of man and his vast store of technical knowledge.

And unlike so many groups in today's world, fireflies aren't out there asking for aid. They aren't running drills to improve their performance. They're not trying to make a statement. They're simply doing their best at being fireflies. It's enough for them.

And its enough for me, too. For, while the fireflies are busy being themselves, their tiny twinkle has the magical power to carry me back to my childhood.

The Tools of the Trade Have Changed

I've been spending quite a bit of time lately, tapping away at my trusty computer, catching up on a number of newspaper columns. And, as I click away, I've come to realize just how fortunate I am to be writing in a time blessed with such advanced tools as my magic Compaq Presario.

As in every field of work, the tools of the writer have undergone amazing changes through the ages. For instance, those of us who try to record the world around us have come a long way from the cave dwellers.

Imagine that first early writer/artist who began painting shapes on the walls of his cave. How did he edit his work?

In the books I've read and the pictures I've seen on the subject, there were no crossed-out horses or painted-over warriors. Instead of the many re-writes I need to put my work into publishable shape, the cave reporter must have been so sure of what he wanted to say that he did it right the first time.

And the early communicator who chiseled his work in stone…did he scratch out his planned project in the dirt first? If so, how did he keep the kids and the family dog from stepping on that original draft of his masterpiece? Such interference could easily have discouraged a budding talent.

As for those who wrote with a quill pen, how did they keep up with the constant demand for paper and ink? There were no Wal-Marts and K-Marts offering an endless supply of blank tablets and throw away ball points.

I can just imagine old Edgar Poe, sitting hunched in concentration at his desk, the oil lamp casting a glow on his furrowed brow. His hand moved across the paper writing carefully, "Quoth the raven"…and then the pen ran out of ink!

The poet, his imagination stopped in mid-flight, would have gone to bed with his thoughts incomplete. For sleepless hours, he would have tossed, waiting impatiently for the dawn. When daylight finally came, he would have hurried next door to borrow a few precious drops of ink. Only then could he sit down and pen the famous ending…"evermore."

My earlier writing days were almost as frustrating. I composed my work directly on a clunky old typewriter. Whenever I faced that blank sheet and aged keyboard, I would expect the worst. The problem was that once the thoughts started rolling, I was unable to control the outpouring of my run away mind. Before long, the ideas and words came faster than I could type. Invariably, on the last line of an otherwise perfect page, I'd introduce a glaring error. The act of tearing the sheet out of the typewriter and starting all over again brought on a physical pain that left me convinced I'd chosen the wrong line of work.

Eventually, some inventive soul who understood such frustration developed the great savior of the writing world, "white out." It allowed me to paint away most of my errors, although the finished piece was a little lumpy here and there.

But now, with the magic computer at my command, a mistake only requires a few strokes of the keyboard to correct. I can't claim this modern genie has made me a better writer, but it has certainly made me a more relaxed one.

I would never have made it as a cave dwelling journalist or a rock chiseling columnist. In my world of multiple assignments and short deadlines, I've found the key to happiness is labeled "delete."

The Family Junk Drawer

I can't avoid it any longer. The time has come to tackle the family junk drawer.

Every household has one of these forgotten corners. It's where the miscellaneous items of life collect undisturbed for years. Yours may be in the side table in the hallway or the bottom drawer of the desk. Or, like ours, it may be in prime kitchen space.

These things are never planned as catch-alls. No one ever says, "Well, Irving, our new kitchen finally has a place for everything. I've decided the silverware will go there, the good china will go here, and this little drawer can be the junk drawer."

No, a real family junk haven just seems to evolve. It's like the one closet in the house where all those never worn but too good to get rid of pieces of clothing congregate out of sight, hoping no one will notice them.

When I was a kid, we didn't actually have a junk DRAWER. Instead, the little china fruit bowl on the dining room table became the place of final rest for a strange assortment of missing items. Of course these things weren't supposed to stay there. We all vowed we'd sort the collection some day and put everything where it really belonged. But sorting day never came.

The bowl was crafted to look like a wicker basket heaped with a variety of almost real fruits: grapes, apples, pears and oranges. And, at the very top, a realistic lemon served as the handle.

As the youngest member of the family, I didn't find the bowl itself half as interesting as it's contents. On a rainy day, I could spend long periods of time happily digging through the stuff that had found its way into this treasure chest.

Ignoring the safety pins and paper clips that sifted themselves to the bottom, I went straight for the random penny or nickel Mom tossed in while cleaning out pockets.

This was also the place to look for the missing piece of a favorite jigsaw puzzle. And when the Monopoly game came up short a hotel or two, we could be pretty sure they were hiding in the fruit bowl.

Then there were the postage stamps. A couple of soaked from the envelope stamps were usually buried among the rubber bands and ticket stubs that lived in the bowl. At one time or another, everyone in the house had raided the lemon-topped refuge for this left over postage. Of course the stamp would be glue-less and wrinkled, but with a dab of paste, it could still take a letter across the country.

I often added a treasure or two to the fruit bowl, just to let the others know I'd been there. My specialties were choice marbles and pretty stones. I don't recall anyone else showing the slightest interest in these items, so my contributions were always there when I went back to retrieve them.

Our current family junk haven is a narrow drawer in the kitchen. It's the official location of the grocery coupon caddy and the resident supply of string. But there are many other things tucked away in its shadowy recesses…tacky refrigerator magnets, lost paper clips, misplaced clothes pins, a selection of random rubber bands.

Actually, there's no telling what has joined the throng in there. And that's why the time has come to confront this demon in our midst. I have to dump the drawer's contents into a big box and begin sorting. Who knows what I'll find.

Come to think of it, I sure could use a couple of extra postage stamps. Do you suppose…?

Nature's Exclamation Point

On a recent warm and breezy night, I was suddenly startled from sleep by a dazzling burst of light.

I caught my breath and lay there, not quite awake, wondering and listening.

Suddenly another flash lit the darkened room with the blaze of mid-day. And, in the distance, the deep voice of thunder rolled across the sleeping countryside.

In a moment, I felt the rush of wind as it tossed the blinds. Then I heard the first tentative tapping of rain drops on the awning above the window. The sound quickly changed to a steady drumming, growing louder and louder.

I got up gently in my still-sleeping house to close the window against the noise and wind. Then I stood looking out at the rain-swept yard.

Through it all, the lightening flashed and the thunder rolled, turning night into day and quiet into chaos.

For me, such demonstrations of nature's majesty are a source of wonder. To watch and listen as the fury unfurls is an awesome experience. The loss of a little sleep is a small price to pay to witness such power.

I've been fascinated by storms all my life. When I feel that special electrical tension in the air that precedes the tumult, I like to find a protected place outside to watch and wait for the opening act. I scan the sky, marveling at the rain-filled slate-colored clouds as they race toward the horizon.

Then come the rolls of thunder and, finally, those first big drops of rain, spattering at my feet, sending me scurrying inside. And accompanying the show, there are the celestial fireworks of the lightning bolts

Through the years, I've come across many bits and pieces of information about the main ingredient of such noisy electrical events, namely lightning.

There are dozens of old sayings dealing with the brilliant flashes that cut the sky. For instance, according to Western American folklore, "Wherever lightning strikes, you will find oil."

Unfortunately, it seems impossible to predict where those bolts will hit. For centuries that unpredictability has caused mankind to devise ways to channel the power of lightning and rob it of its potential for destruction. From lightning rods perched atop old barns to surge protectors for computer equipment, whole industries have sprung up in an attempt to keep lightning in its place.

But on the night of the recent storm, as I stood by the window and watched the flashes change darkness to daylight, I wasn't thinking of any of the bits of lightning information I've collected over the years. Instead, I was simply a spectator, watching and listening to the awesome power of nature as she marched across the land, proclaiming her majesty with a summer storm.

June is a Month of Turning Points

If the road of life came with a map, it would carry a warning in bold letters: Be prepared for frequent, unexpected course changes.

June is often a prime time for such bends in the road. Graduations, weddings, welcoming a baby…all forever alter the pathway ahead. But, though these events mean major life-changing adjustments, they are not the kind of turning points that catch us unaware. We have plenty of time to plan for such happy transitions.

The changes that take us by surprise are those subtle, quiet direction shifts we all have along the way. These rarely arrive with whistles and bells. No one holds up a sign beside our road of life saying, "Pay attention, This is important!"

We seldom realize, until long after the event, that a certain moment, a chance meeting, a sudden insight was one of those life-will-never-be-the-same experiences.

If you think back to when you met your mate, chances are there were no flashing lights above his or her head spelling out "This is the one."

And, when something drew you to a certain career or field of work, there was nothing to indicate this could become your daily activity for the years ahead.

From jobs and hobbies, from community involvements to political causes, most of the projects that make up our day-to-day lives began with some unannounced turning point. In almost every case, we came to a fork in our pathway. The decision we made moved us on in one direction, leaving behind the "road not taken."

I've been thinking about my own turning points lately, and I realize that, as with each of us, the course adjustments I've made have added up to who and where I am today.

Meeting a newly-discharged airman in Fort Worth, Texas, led to 47 wonderful years of marriage.

A class at Chautauqua opened the door to a long-dreamed-of career in writing.

Accepting an editor's challenge to write a personal experience column has given me the matchless opportunity to "Mosey Along" with you every week.

Day-by-day, we each come to turning points such as these. You might find it an interesting exercise to think back over your own turning points. You'll probably see, as I did, that many of these important events slipped by so quietly you hardly noticed your pathway had been forever changed.

This month, many folks will be making such life-changing transitions. The June graduations and weddings are the kinds of course adjustments that bring long-awaited joy.

But, for all of us, our way is frequently dotted with quiet life-altering course changes. Yet these surprises are what make each day so exciting.

Just remember to stay alert. Maybe you'll be able to identify some of those turning points that are sure to come along as you travel your own road of life.

Hardware Names Can Boggle the Mind

Many years ago, when we operated a small town Mom-and-Pop hardware store, we learned first hand how difficult it is for the average shopper to name the piece of hardware he or she is looking for. The vocabulary of the hardware business in not exactly user friendly.

Almost daily some poor soul would come through the door with a purposeful look on his face. He'd march up and down the aisles, scanning first one side, then the other. Finally, overwhelmed by the sheer numbers of things displayed, the confused customer would make his way to the counter.

"I need an adapter," he'd say, glancing helplessly around the store.

George, the ever-patient hardware man, would then repeat the most often asked question in the hardware business. "What do you want to do with it?"

"Well," the customer would say, "I want to plug a plug into a plug."

"Sounds like a grounding adapter," George would announce, directing the man to the electrical department.

That was one of the easier problems to solve. Often waiting on customers in a hardware store is like playing 20 Questions.

"Would that be a plumbing, electrical or telephone item?"

"Do you want it galvanized or plain?"

"Interior or exterior?" "Latex or oil based?"

For the average customer, the maze can be intimidating.

To make their shopping easier, many entered the store clutching small bits of paper bearing detailed descriptions of their needs.

We often waited on women, for instance, who had been given what they thought were exact instructions by their husbands. The men, always in the middle of a job, were waiting in a ditch, under a sink, or beside the furnace. It was a time of high stress for the wife.

"I need a pipe fitting," the lady would say, reading directly from her fact sheet. You could tell by her stance and her tone that this time she was sure she'd be able to bring home the right part.

"Plastic or galvanized?" George would ask patiently.

"Uh, plastic," she'd say, consulting the paper.

"And what size would that be?"

"Three inch," she'd reply, feeling more confident by the minute.

George would lead the customer to the display filled with the three inch pipe and fittings used for drain installation.

"Did you want schedule 30 or schedule 40?" he'd ask.

Suddenly the lady's air of confidence would vanish. With nothing on the paper to indicate the answer to the question, she would have to follow the path of many before her. She'd call home.

Customers routinely came in with requests for "doohickeys", "whatchamacallits" and "thingamajigs". It was a constant challenge to help them find what they needed.

In a store that carries such odd items as oakum, cold shuts and snakes, it's little wonder labels become major stumbling blocks.

And, to make matters worse, many items used for different purposes have the same names. Clamps, adapters, couplers, brackets, connectors…it's enough to boggle the mind.

In addition to the simply confusing, the hardware store is also filled with the slightly embarrassing. For example, most ladies found it difficult to ask for a stud finder.

But it was the terminology used for plumbing and electrical items that I took exception to. The departments were filled with male and female fittings, couplings, and adapters. During our hardware years I launched a personal and unsuccessful campaign to change the names to "goes-intas" and "goes-outas". The idea never caught on.

But what can you expect from an industry that insists on selling galvanized nipples and bastard files?

Check Your Plimsoll Line

Life in today's world is a constant balancing act, especially for women.

Magazines, movies, newspaper…everything we see and hear…all try to convince us that we are capable of being real life versions of Wonder Woman, if only we are willing to try hard enough. We've come to expect ourselves to be the perfect wife, mother, employee, church member, community volunteer, etc., etc.

When frustration and exhaustion set in, disillusionment quickly follows. We finally have to admit that excelling at everything is simply not possible. No one can do it all.

I've been through the course more often than I care to remember. Each time I let myself get caught up in taking on more than I can possibly accomplish, I convince myself that THIS time, determination will help me to pull it off.

It never works.

I've finally resigned myself to the fact that I am simply not Wonder Woman material. And, I've decided that's just fine.

Some time ago, I read about a man who understood what can happen when you take on more than you can carry. You may never have heard of Samuel Plimsoll, but he could teach us all something about how to keep life from getting out of hand.

Mr. Plimsoll was an Englishman who lived just over a century ago. He was interested in ships and the people who sailed them.

After long observation, Plimsoll became convinced many of the ships that sank, and many of the lives that were lost at sea, were the result of overloading the vessels.

He took his concerns to Parliament and finally convinced the law makers to do something to correct the problem. Due to his efforts, ship owners were required to paint a danger mark on the sides of their vessels to indicate when they were loaded beyond a safe limit.

That line, known as the Plimsoll Line, is still used by seafaring men today. Every registered ship carries the mark, giving a visual limit to the load the vessel can safely carry.

Reading about the Plimsoll Line made me realize that we could all use such a guide for our lives.

It's so easy to become overloaded by the demands of work, family, and community. We each need a clear idea of what our limits are. And we need the courage to say "no" when things begin to overwhelm us.

We owe it to ourselves, our families and our friends to keep an eye on our own "waterline." We have to be sure not to take on a cargo of responsibilities that could sink us.

So how's your Plimsoll Line?

A Family Treasure is Fading Away

The old screen door, that long time gateway to the home, is in danger of extinction.

With the advent of the attractive and efficient aluminum storm door, the screen door most of us knew as kids has fallen into that vast wasteland of not quite an antique. And, with the replacement of the old wooden door by those fancy aluminum units, we've lost a unsung participant in the ongoing drama of family life.

I still remember the door-closing techniques of the various members of our family.

Dad's return from work was always punctuated with an authoritative slam of the door, followed by the announcement to anyone within ear shot, "I'm home!" It was the acknowledged pre-dinner call to the family. We knew within fifteen minutes the evening meal would be on the table.

Unlike Dad's entrance, when my sister was trying to sneak in late from a date, the door would open and close almost silently. Almost. But, with the acute hearing of the parent on duty, Mom detected the all but imperceptible squeak of the door hinges and was instantly on her feet.

When my brothers returned from a hard day of being teenagers, the door always closed with a resounding bang. That arresting sound was quickly followed by an urgent, "What's for dinner?"

For my part, as the youngest in the tribe I found the screen door simply a minor obstacle between me and the vast outside world. My

only thought was to pass as quickly as possible from in to out. Whatever happened to the screen door during the passage, so be it.

Given all this coming and going, slamming and banging, even a
brand new screen door began to sag in a short time.

Fortunately, each of these important entrance protectors was
equipped with a heavy rod running diagonally from an upper corner to
the opposite lower one. The rod had a sturdy turnbuckle in the center.
By turning the turnbuckle the right number of times, even a badly
drooping door could be squared up. Ours, as I recall, needed frequent
adjusting.

Then, there was the screen itself. With such important items as ten-
nis rackets, footballs, brooms, yardsticks and the occasional running
child constantly colliding with the metal mesh, holes soon appeared
that were spacious enough to admit large families of flies, traveling in
formation.

When this happened, Dad, or one of the boys, would cut a small
piece of spare screening, bend the tiny metal ends of the wire and push
the patch against the hole. Then it was a simple matter to go to the
other side of the door and bend the protruding ends flat against the
screen. It made for an effective, if not attractive, cover for the tear. In
time, our screen was a patch-work of repairs, each site recalling a lapse
in caution.

Most families installed what was considered a state-of-the-art security system on their screen doors. These hook-and-eye latches were,
and still are, readily available from the local hardware store. The less-
than-intimidating lock was little match for an adult who wanted to
enter. A really hard tug, administered by a grown-up determined to get
in, would usually pull one of the sections of the latch from its mount
on door or jamb.

Though it didn't hinder adults, the hook-and-eye lock was very
effective against children. One of our often-repeated family stories
involves just such a situation. The tale, handed down for at least two

generations, involved Mom's little sister, Virginia and their straight-laced Aunt Rose.

Rose, an overly cautious, single lady of advanced years, always made a habit of latching the screen against imagined intruders. She followed this routine whether she was at home or staying with relatives.

At the time, little Virginia, was a child of 4 or 5. As with most kids of that age, she hated to stop playing for anything less than a full-blown emergency. She often waited to answer the call of nature until the last moment. Then it was a mad dash to the house. One day, the story goes, Aunt Rose was visiting. As was her habit, she made sure the screen was latched as soon as the children went out to play.

Virginia, responding at the last instant to nature's call, rushed to the door, only to find it locked. She yelled and pounded in frustration until Aunt Rose came to investigate.

There, standing in a slowly growing puddle, was Virginia, sobbing accusingly, "You see what you made me do!"

And another family drama was etched in memory, thanks to that vanishing treasure, the old screen door.

Beating the Heat

The burning question on everyone's lips these days is "How do you survive this heat?" One of the most popular answers is that dear old summertime standard, the fan.

I remember the ones that sustained us during the blistering Texas summers of my childhood. These fans were cumbersome metal affairs that swiveled noisily while delivering their welcome breeze.

On days when the thermometer read 100 plus, you could find the family clustered around the relief giving fans, reading the funny papers or listening to the "Jack Benny Show" or "Lux Radio Theater." Even though the air was hot, it didn't feel so stifling as long as it was moving.

A lifelong fan of fans, I have my personal list of favorites. Near the top are the fold-up Oriental styles you hold in your hand. I always carry one in my purse for use in stuffy waiting rooms and lecture halls. I've noticed some strange glances when I unfold my little fan, but these turn to envy as the breezes begin to swirl around me.

Although many families have taken the leap into air conditioning, you can't beat fans for efficient and economical cooling. And they fit into every location. For instance, we have several desk toppers. Here at the computer, one cools me as I write. I think of this little blue bladed air mover as my portable breeze and carry it with me around the house.

This year, we installed several ceiling fan/lights. We found the hardest part of adding these was choosing among the hundreds of styles and colors. There are fan/lights for every home from a cottage to a castle.

Of course the list of fans also includes varieties for the window, above the stove and in the attic. There just seems to be no end of the ways devised to get rid of hot air and stir up a little breeze. At this time of year, all of them are welcome.

But, as much as I enjoy the benefits of fans, I can remember one experience that dulled my enthusiasm. It happened during the last sweltering weeks of my senior year in high school. I had spent hours organizing notes for my term paper. The dining room table was spread with more than a dozen carefully categorized piles of cards and bits of paper.

As I put the last stack in order, Mom came in. She took a look at my perspiring, flushed face and said, "How can you stand the heat in here?" With one quick motion she stepped to the far end of the table and turned on the fan.

The View from Beneath
the Boom

Over the years, our boating experiences have taking us from Lake Erie to Findley Lake, from Chautauqua Lake to the waters of Charlotte Harbor in Florida. And, as time has passed, I've come to accept a great truth: our three-member family crew is made up of two fearless sailors and one chicken. I'm the chicken.

To my credit, I've spent years perfecting my role as the Captain's wife and First mate.

I've learned to refer to the pointy end of the boat as "the bow." I've mastered the meaning of such nautical terms as "port," "starboard" and "ready about." And I've discovered from hard experience why that big swingy thing at the bottom of the mainsail is called the "boom."

I can throw a nutritious lunch into a canvas bag in less than three minutes, efficiently handle cast-off duties and even understand why every captain, including mine, yearns for a larger boat.

In fact, as long as the wind is blowing at 10 knots or less, a larger boat even sounds good to me. On a lazy day of gentle breezes, I easily share the joy my husband, Captain George, and son, Tim, feel in being out on the water. Under a cornflower blue sky hung with cotton-ball clouds, the water kicking up diamonds in our wake, life and sailing are sweet and satisfying.

My problem comes when the winds begin to gust to gale force.

As the gentle waves turn to white caps and the boat's quiet glide increases to a gallop, the men of the crew congratulate each other with, "Now we're SAILING!" Faces wreathed in smiles, they squint into the mounting fury, giggling like schoolkids as the spray breaks across the bow.

I, however, crouch low, trying to escape the onslaught as I clutch a boat cushion with white-knuckled grip. Soon I find myself fighting some primal urge to suck my thumb and whimper, "Mommy!"

After a while, the Captain becomes aware of the slouched figure try-ing desperately to curl into a fetal position. Then, in tribute to more than 40 years of marriage, he relents and lets out enough sail to bring the mast up a few degrees from its near-horizontal position.

The valiant boat responds by straightening slightly, giving me a reviving moment or two to breathe again.

Fortunately, not all of our cruises involve such traumatic scenes. Often, if the wind doesn't gust too strongly and the waves behave, I cope rather well, for a chicken put out to sea.

In fact, through the years…between bouts of sheer terror…I've managed to gather some wonderful memories while dodging the boom.

The one that stands out most clearly was our "hat overboard emer-gency."

Like most men, my Captain had a favorite hat. Actually, calling this poor, worn, faded scrap of blue cotton a "hat" stretches the word far past what the dictionary had in mind. Put bluntly, it was a disgrace. But no amount of coaxing would convince the skipper it was time to replace his longtime favorite head covering.

On this particular day, the breeze was perfect, the sailing just my style. And, at the helm of his trusty boat, the Captain sat in complete control, his faded, torn hat jauntily perched on his head.

Suddenly a freak gust of wind caught us from behind, and in an instant the hat sailed off that proud head, landing several yards away, off the starboard beam. The old rag seemed destined for a watery grave.

Now as any sailor can tell you, turning a sailboat under sail requires time and space. And here, within sight but settling fast, the captain's favorite hat was rapidly running out of both.

Somehow, with masterful sailing techniques born of experience and inspired by desperation, the Captain heroically turned the boat and sailed back to retrieve his prize.

I was certain the faded mess would sink below the waves before we reached it. But, miraculously, the sodden thing stayed afloat until son Tim reached overboard and scooped it from the water.

The Captain was overjoyed.

I secretly vowed to have a private talk with my son about the value of letting nature take its course.

I hate to say it, but I'm afraid a wife overboard emergency might not have resulted in as fast a response. Still, to the Captain's credit, I'm sure I would have been saved…eventually. I think he realizes our three-member crew isn't complete without the comic relief of a chicken sailor who can pack a lunch on short notice.

The Family Chef Never Stops Learning

Unless you were an accomplished cook before becoming the head of your own kitchen, chances are you discovered early on that the path from the cook book to the table is often paved with broken dreams.

When I married, my cooking background was limited to time spent at my mother's side, learning to make a few favorite dishes. But I seldom took responsibility for an entire meal. I could eventually whip up a tasty dish of scalloped potatoes. But Mom would pull the meal together by handling the complexities of all the other items on the menu…salad, meat dish, vegetables, dessert.

Yet, inevitably, the day came when I found myself alone in my own kitchen, a bride unprepared for the role of chef.

Our doll house of an apartment was tucked above the double garage of a large home. The heart of our tiny hide away was a cozy knotty pine kitchen. In spite of its size, this cooking center was equipped with the smaller version of all the appliances necessary to feed a hungry husband.

So with the positive outlook of a new bride overshadowing my lack of experience, I put on the frilly embroidered apron I had received as a wedding gift and began my career as the chief cook for our family of two.

The first few meals were a rousing success. With a breakfast menu of cereal, toast and juice, I was off to a great start. The toast did come out a little darker than I had expected, but a few scrapes with a knife, followed by a liberal dose of jam, made it passable.

Lunch was generally of the sandwich variety. No problem there.

At supper time I began using more creativity. Study sessions with my new cook books and some advanced planning gave me the confidence to try a few casseroles. I even made an acceptable dish of macaroni and cheese.

The successes of my first week of meals lulled me into a false feeling of security. How tough could it be? I had easy-to-follow recipes, a shiny new set of cook ware and a husband with a good appetite and a forgiving stomach. I was on my way to the Betty Crocker hall of fame.

With a feeling of invincibility, I decided the time had come to invite our first supper guests to join us. It was a major step forward in our new life.

It took me almost a week to decide on our first guests. The size of the apartment required I limit the list to two. My groom and I finally chose the two people we wanted most to impress with our glowing domesticity: my mother and his best friend, a bachelor named Bill.

After more thought than they give to planning a White House banquet, I decided on the components of this red letter meal. The salad would be followed by creamy mashed potatoes, tasty breaded pork chops and some special herb laced green beans.

I would even make some from scratch custard for dessert.

When the fateful evening arrived, our guests showed up an hour before the meal, eager to see how we were doing. Since the apartment was essentially one large room, they sat at the table and watched me as I worked.

I noticed the lettuce for the salad was well-passed its prime at just about the time the potatoes boiled over, leaving the top of the stove a disaster. The new can opener refused to attack the lid of the green bean can and I realized I had also forgotten the herbs I needed to turn them into a special dish. And, to add to the confusion, the pan I was heating for the pork chops began to smoke menacingly.

Mom, who had vowed not to interfere, sat watching the show with quiet understanding.

And I, in my now stained apron, began to accept the fact that things were not going well.

It was almost an hour later that I was able to deliver the meal to the table. Although we were all famished by this time, and our guests tried valiantly to find positive things to say about the food, it was obvious I had fallen far short of whipping up the perfect feast.

The potatoes were cold by the time the pork chops were ready (though somewhat smokey). The green beans went from can to pan to table with no intervention from me. And the custard never got past the planning stage.

Fortunately, we had some cookies I had bought at the store. For some reason, they were a huge hit and quickly disappeared. That's something I can't say for the rest of the food.

Although I have come a long way since that disastrous early meal, it taught me a few memorable lessons. First, there are some things you don't find in any cook book. And second, being the family chef is an ongoing learning experience.

A Slice of American Pie

On a recent sun-drenched Saturday, I was running errands when I stopped at the corner of East Whallon and South Erie Street in our little hometown of Mayville, New York.

Cars, trucks and vans of every description lined the street on both sides. When I turned north, I saw the reason for the crowds. At St. Paul's Episcopal Church, on the west side of the street, dozens of folks were moving slowly among benches and tables laden with rummage sale items. And, toward the back of the property, a grill sizzled with fragrant hot dogs at the edge of a refreshment tent. Beside the hot dog area, a table of home made pies invited attention.

Across the street, the front lawn of the Mayville library sported a bright yellow and white tent. Under the canopy, tables laden with hundreds of books were set out for the final day of the library's annual book sale. Clusters of book lovers took advantage of the cool, shady setting to scan the tables or stand sampling one of the many volumes available at bargain prices.

Up the street from the library, the Quality Market parking lot was a constantly-changing panorama of shoppers coming and going. Moms with kids in tow loaded heaping bags into their waiting cars. Dads stopped in for a last minute addition to the family's picnic preparations. Couples pushed filled carts across the pavement to their waiting vans. The weekly grocery rush was on.

Across from the Market, Mayville Hardware had a steady stream of folks going in with long lists and coming out with paint and brushes, bags of screws and nails, hammers and screw drivers...all manner of materials for this fix-up season of the year.

Other businesses along Erie Street also drew their share of browsers and buyers. In short, it was a typical Main Street style day in this grass-roots piece of small town America.

When I completed my own list of stops, I headed back down South Erie Street and once again took in this special summertime scene.

A homeowner in paint spattered jeans wielded his brush methodically, coating the front of his home with a bright new coat to welcome the season.

Kids on roller blades whisked along the sidewalks. A flower filled planter swung in the breeze at the edge of one of the broad porches fronting a spacious two-story home behind century old maples.

And at the foot of the hill, I could see the spread of the sun sparkled lake. Off in the distance, the sails of a pair of sailboats skimmed above the water like two matched crescents.

Before I turned off of South Erie Street toward home, I slowed for a closer look around me. I couldn't help feeling that tucked away in some quiet corner of the scene, there must be a Norman Rockwell look-alike, brushes in hand, capturing this piece of American pie on canvas.

The Lure of Porches

As July smiles its way toward August, porches are the best place to be.

This is the time of year when out side is so much more inviting than in. The time when a cool drink, a shaded porch and friendly conversation are all part of the summertime picture.

Back in February, when the winds were howling and the snow turned the frozen world into a white-on-white landscape, the porch was a desolate place. But in July and August, there's no better spot for relaxing, spinning dreams or sharing stories than that most inviting spot, the porch.

Just so we understand what we're talking about here, Webster defines a porch as a "covered entrance." I've always thought of a real, home style porch as being on the front of the house. This special place has a roof and some comfortable chairs. Hanging baskets, tables and swings are optional.

In our corner of the world, porches hold a rightful place of honor in the scheme of things. From lakeside cottages in Mayville to expensive retreats in Chautauqua Institution, from farm houses in Clymer and Sherman to regal two-story homes along Westfield's main street, porches are treasured features at this outdoor time of year.

Some are wicker-chaired wonders. Others are tiny affairs with webbed aluminum seating. But whatever the size and furnishings, a porch acts as a magnet, drawing folks outside to relax with a good book or good friends, both equally prized in Chautauqua County.

Unfortunately, more recent trends in home building have done away with such useful and attractive front of the house assets as the porch. Today, throughout America, the natural wood deck has taken over as the preferred outdoor living space. But, unlike a porch, the deck is usually at the back of the home, and seldom covered. That may make it a great spot to sit in the sun and watch your own backyard. But, on the down side, the deck doesn't let you see what's going on in the street out front, nor for that matter, who's visiting the folks next door. Front porches are definitely more neighbor-friendly structures than back decks.

Because of its location at the front of the house, the old-fashioned porch continues to have a unique place in the life of the family. 'Most everything that happens, happens across the porch.

The young bride crosses the porch to take her place as the lady of the house. The expectant woman waddles slowly from the front door to the steps as she leaves for the hospital. The young mother and father bring their newborn babies home across the porch. And as the children grow, rain showers, as well as the blistering days of summer, find them gathered on the porch to play. Young couples sit and talk, hold hands and share a first kiss on the porch swing.

A porch is only a structure, only a part of the house. But, it's also a place of quiet voices rising and falling at twilight, a spot for solitary contemplation, a focus for family fun. In short, it's the perfect outdoor room for relaxing away the lazy days of summer.

The Lesson of the Rose

Like all youngsters, my childhood was filled with endless commands to "be patient," and admonitions of "you'll just have to wait!"

Mom constantly tried to slow me down. But, even though she would lovingly assure me that Christmas, Easter, my birthday, the circus...or whatever, would come in time. I was sure the days and hours would never pass. It was an uphill battle for her, until the lesson of the rose.

The incident was one of those small, undramatic experiences that happen quietly throughout a lifetime, one of those moments when somehow our view of the world is subtly changed forever.

During my childhood years, we had an old and stately white rose beside the porch. The bush was not generous with blooms, but each one was magnificent.

When a rare bud would appear, I watched its painfully slow development with growing impatience. Every morning, I would rush to the porch, expecting to see the lovely rose at last opening its petals to me. But the progress was so gradual it seemed the bud would forever be only a bud.

One dry summer, the roses were especially scarce. With growing expectation, I kept an eager eye on a single perfect bud. Week after week, it hardly seemed to change. The development was so slow, it was as if the bud was made of painted porcelain. Would I ever see the ivory velvet of that beautiful promise?

Finally, my limited patience could stand no more. I took matters into my own hands. While the rest of the family was busy with less important concerns than roses, I got Mom's scissors from the sewing drawer. Quietly, I went out to the porch and cut the bud from the bush.

Hiding the tightly closed flower behind me, I slipped into the empty kitchen. With no one around to interrupt, I took the big butcher knife from the drawer and expectantly cut the bud open. I knew inside I would find a tiny, but perfect rose, waiting to be liberated.

But instead, there was only a pile of small, softly folded petals. Even in the center of the bud's tight little fist, I found no rose.

My disappointment was overwhelming. Not only did my dream rose not exist, I had destroyed one of the rare chances I had to enjoy the special beauty offered by the rose bush.

No one in the family seemed to miss the bud. At least nothing was ever said. But, for days I mourned the loss.

I've never forgotten that tiny rose-in-the-making that never bloomed.

I can't claim that I've conquered impatience. It still seems Christmas takes a very long time to come. And it's never easy to wait quietly throughout the long and blustery winter for spring to arrive.

But, I've at least learned to let my roses bloom in their own time.

Stacks of Paper, Piles of Pens

I'm hanging on these days, but just barely.

My problem is that I'm overwhelmed when stores begin their back-to-school sales. It's not the clothing or the colorful back packs that do me in. No, it's all that paper, all those pens.

I have this weird compulsion to grab a stack of blank, inviting notebooks and run off to some quiet corner to create. In my weaker moments I'm convinced that with the right pen and a lined notebook, I could scribble off some deathless prose that would wow the world.

Even the reams of clean, white paper seem to be whispering to me, inviting the touch of my eager inner word smith.

This seasonal addiction is nothing new. I've always loved school supplies.

I can recall those long ago days when my elementary school classmates and I prepared for our annual return to classes. The school sent out lists of the supplies each student should bring along on that first day.

With list in hand, I dragged Mom into the five-and-dime for our August buying trip. Somehow I managed to turn the simple project into a marathon. Even my ever-patient Mom became antsy as I dawdled among the inviting offerings.

A number of the items were required by the school system. No room here for individuality. Among these necessities were those official penmanship tablets with the black binding at the top. The red or brown covers contained the entire alphabet in cursive writing. I was inspired by the grace and beauty of those well-formed letters. But, alas, even with hours of push-pull and circle drawing exercises, my letters never approached the perfection displayed on the tablet cover.

If the writing tablets allowed no choice, the stacks of spiral notebooks offered something different for everyone. It was here I loved to browse for long periods of time. Unfortunately, these spirals and the packages of three hole notebook paper were meant only for the "older" kids.

My brother, ten years my senior, and my sister, five years older than I, were my role models of cool school kids.

Each year Mom bought them fresh, clean three-ring binders. The notebooks were made with a tough, cloth like covering that resembled a light blue denim.

As soon as they got their new notebooks home, Alan and Lynn set about turning their pristine notebooks into their individualized declarations of independence. Their personal "works of art" were carefully splashed across the notebook face with colored pencils or pens. Today's vivid magic markers had not come along at that time, but our family artists weren't hindered. Their resources were more than a match for the plain blue backgrounds that provided their canvas for these creative expressions. In no time, the notebooks reflected the special flair of the owner. It could never be lost in a pile of similar binders.

Sadly, I was far too young for the notebook set. But I found my greatest shopping enjoyment when our supply buying session moved into the crayon section.

Nothing so excited my imagination as those beautiful boxes of perfectly-formed Crayola Crayons. Each year I begged Mom for the largest carton we could afford. One August I actually managed to convince her I needed a box with three rows of colors. This treasure even had its own built-in crayon sharpener. It was like driving to second grade in a BMW while my classmates had to settle for used Fords.

Today's school students will return to classrooms far different from the simple ones of my day. And there won't be any penmanship tablets on their list of back-to-class equipment. Instead, their learning environment will include computers and high-tech teaching aids.

But there is still a need for spiral notebooks and colored pens. Stacks of these necessities, along with the latest boxes of Crayola Crayons, are once again filling the stores.

It's enough to send a school supply addict into a panic.

So much paper, so many pens, so little time.

The Strange World of Fog

The world was wrapped in a muffler of fog this morning.

Fog fascinates me.

That may seem strange to those who have spent a lifetime here in the lush, moisture rich Great Lakes area. I, on the other hand, was raised in the vast, often dusty dry state of Texas.

In my growing up years, I saw fog only two or three times. It was such a rarity that neighbors and family members phoned one another to call attention to the strange phenomenon.

The moisture content of the Texas air was so low that, even at the height of a rain storm, humidity would reach only 50 per cent or so.

So, even after 30 years here, where a such an earth-bound cloud is a common occurrence, fog still intrigues me.

This morning I took an early walk in this strangely softened world. The fog closed around and moved with me like a silent companion.

All the familiar outlines were blurred, as if seen through a smoky lens. Everything took on a misty quality. The haze gave even the common things an uncommon loveliness.

Spider webs, stretched on fences and mailbox posts, were transformed in the fog. Decorated with pearls of moisture along their intricate structures, they looked like jewel-studded Christmas tree ornaments.

Even the weeds in the ditches had a soft glow, giving them a mysterious beauty.

The fog not only affected the look of the world. Sounds were different, too. The strident cry of an unseen blue jay became a whispered whistle. The clatter of passing cars turned to a subdued rumble.

And the dimensions of my familiar neighborhood seemed reduced in the fog. Instead of the usual clear view of where I'd been and where I was going, my vision was limited to a short distance before and behind me. Somehow it helped me focus my thinking on the moment, as though past and future, both out of sight, were also beyond my concern.

Now, in the late morning sun, the fog has disappeared. The world has returned to its familiar, sharply defined shapes of trees and telephone poles, gardens and garages.

Life is clearer in the unclouded light of a bright day. There is less mystery, more certainty.

But I can be sure that as summer deepens, I'll soon wake to another fog shrouded dawn. And for a former child of the dry southwest, the fascination will be there once again.

I'm a Quilt Lover

My fascination with quilts was launched some years ago when I dropped in at a show featuring more than 30 of the hand-made coverlets. I'd seen photos in magazines, but nothing had prepared me for the intricate detail and stunning beauty of the treasures on display. The show included both heirloom pieces and newly completed creations. I was in awe.

Through the years, I've come to realize there's a vast sisterhood that shares my quilt fascination. Some collect them, others spend countless hours styling and stitching them. Unfortunately, I haven't the money nor the time for either. But I still consider myself a quilt lover.

There's something about these colorful coverlets that strikes a universal cord in most women. It's a comfortable sort of feeling combining the appeal of sheets line-drying in the sun and the cozy homines of sewing by the fire on a winter night.

When I discovered the wonderful world of quilting I began making routine stops at a quilt shop near work. I whiled away countless lunch breaks just browsing among the store's ever-changing selection of fabrics.

Thanks to my new found enthusiasm, I bought dozens of quilt magazines and pattern books. Each was filled with creations I wanted to duplicate. But, as with so many good intentions, lack of time shot down my plans.

Eventually, I was able to complete a few small projects.

During my string quilting phase, I stitched up several vests for my daughters. These fashion accessories were very popular at the time. The girls wore them proudly for a couple of years. Now I imagine, the vests are tucked away in the corners of closets devoted to more current fashions. But making them was an enjoyable activity. It gave me the chance to play with color and pattern combinations on a small scale.

But, though I've never had the dedication to complete a full size quilt, luck brought a very special one into our lives. It's become a prize the whole family has shared.

Years ago, I worked in a nursing home in Erie, PA. One fall, as I went about my duties, I watched with interest the progress of a project undertaken by some of the home's more active ladies. Each week, these delightful women got together for quilting sessions. Their eyes were dimming and their fingers were knotted by arthritis. Still, they all enjoyed the long-familiar activities of stitching and chatting.

At the start of their work, they carefully studied the fabrics available for the project, then each chose a combination that pleased her. As the weeks went on, the group concentrated on hand-sewing small fabric squares into larger quilt blocks.

These were not the kind of quilt blocks featured on the glossy pages of quilting magazines. Several of the finished pieces combined scraps of patterned polyester with flower-printed cotton.

Others had a beige corduroy stitched to a blue seersucker. A few paired a light woolen blend with a work-weight twill.

But sewn into the quilt blocks were the final creative efforts of many delightful women, ladies I had come to know and love.

The quilt was offered through a fund-raising raffle at Christmas time. With no expectations of winning, I bought a chance for a quarter. Amazingly, when the lucky ticket was drawn, it was mine.

Through the years this one-of-a-kind quilt has given comfort to the kids as they recovered from the flu, warmed my husband as he napped on a chilly winter evening and relieved my discomfort when my leg was in a cast.

This unusual hand-made blanket doesn't look at all like the handsome creations that captured my heart at that long ago quilt show. Yet it does have two things in common with most hand-crafted quilts of old. It was fashioned by women who had devoted their entire lives to their homes and families. And it was made from whatever scraps of fabric were available.

As with so many treasured quilts of the past, the hands that crafted our comfortable old coverlet are now stilled and at peace. That, after all, is part of the lovely legacy of quilts. They preserve the caring and creativity of a generation and hold it in trust for the future.

The Aromas of Autumn

A couple of weeks ago, our family trio took time out to savor an end-of-summer day of sun and warm breezes. The sky was a sparkling blue, decorated with white cloud towers as we headed north toward the vineyards of grape country along the Lake Erie shoreline.

But, even before we reached Westfield, the car was engulfed in the heady, musky "purplish" perfume of ripe grapes.

In a vineyard beside Plank Road, a giant blue grape picker lumbered along, straddling the rows of vines to harvest the rich, jewel-like bunches. Nearby, a tractor pulled a trailer loaded with crates, waiting to take the treasure away for processing into juices and jellies. And everywhere hung that sweet, indescribable smell of fresh, sun-warmed grapes.

I first inhaled that matchless perfume over forty years ago, when I came to this area in our second year of marriage. Since that original introduction to the autumn aroma of sun-ripened grapes waiting for the picking, I have been addicted to these seasonal trips to the vineyards.

When our children were small, we made it a family project each year at grape-harvest season, to visit one of the "pick-your-own" farms. Here, armed with splint baskets, we would march along the rows of grape vines, taking off large bunches of the beautiful purple or red grapes and dropping them into the waiting baskets. The kids never got many. They were too busy nibbling as they went along. As we gathered back at the car and loaded the trunk with our heaping baskets, we would all stop for a moment and take deep breaths of the aroma wafting from those glistening globes of grapes.

Now, even though we no longer have the need, nor the space, for the canning sessions of old, I still make sure we take our seasonal drive to the vineyards. It has become a must-do part of our fall activities.

And on this day, as in all those past grape-harvest seasons, I took in great gulps of air, trying to fill myself with that magnificent scent. Before long, I was growing dizzy from the deep breathing. But I didn't want to miss a moment of this unforgettable experience.

We drove on to Route 5, where more vineyards stretched away from the road, soaking up the sun and giving off their warm, earthy perfume. The odor was intoxicating.

How I wish I could bottle that wonderful aroma. Then on the inevitable days when the house is closed against the cold and rain, I could spray it around. With a deep breath of the scent, I could close my eyes and savor again the sight of lush grape vines rustling in the warm breeze, the look of a fresh bunch of Concords just picked from beneath the sheltering leaves, and the feel of the dirt path under my feet.

Learning to See With a Pencil

My neighbor, Sally, is a retired art teacher. But, like many educators who simply can't pack their gift for sharing knowledge away, Sally just keeps on teaching. Whether it's in a classroom at the local Arts Center or with a single pupil in a one-on-one setting, Sally finds endless pleasure in helping others to see the world through the eyes of the artist.

She recently took on another student, a senior soul seeking to learn how to draw.

That student is me.

Sally's first advice set the tone for all that will undoubtedly follow on this journey of discovery. She said simply, "Learning to draw begins with learning to see."

With that, she set me up in a comfortable chair with a soft pencil and a fresh sheet of paper clipped to a drawing board.

On the table before me, Sally arranged a long strip of masking tape which she coiled and twisted, stretched and looped in a free form flow. For the next two hours, with frequent encouragement from my mentor, I worked to see and sketch the tape.

"Look for the loops and curves," Sally said. "Watch the way the lines come forward then fall back. Pay attention to the patterns of shadow and light."

I would love to report that when I got up from that first exercise, I had captured a tiny portion of what Sally calls the "essence" of what I saw. But, alas, my tape looked flat and lifeless. Yet there were curves here and there that actually suggested the little scene I had been studying.

The most important advancement I took away with me from the first session was a new excitement in seeing the world more clearly through the use of my pencil.

I'm still in the most basic portion of my drawing education. Following Sally's suggestion, between our lessons together I'm working on my own on some "samplers" of small items.

The other day, I spent a few delightful hours sketching a small apothecary jar and a pencil holder. Amazingly, the drawing of the jar shows some depth and perspective. I think the "portrait" of this simple item could actually be recognized for what it was meant to be.

My rendition of the pencil holder, however, had major flaws. But, using those deficiencies as teaching tools, Sally gently showed me how to improve the composition. Once again, she taught me how to see with my pencil.

I'm currently working on a real challenge. It's a lovely piece of driftwood. When she placed it on the table, Sally carefully pointed out the hollows and highlights, the sweep of the curves and the textures of the weathered wood.

Under Sally's practiced eye and careful analysis, what had seemed only a simple piece of water-tossed wood became a unique and intricate treasure of nature.

I've been trying to capture the essence of that piece of driftwood for several days. So far, my drawing, for the most part, is still flat and lifeless.

Yet in one turn of a weathered twig, at one small overlapping of two lines, in a tiny hollow near the center, there are bits and pieces of the whole that are starting to resemble the original.

Little by little, through my pencil I'm beginning to see!

Adventures in Driving

In our society, the act of driving represents much more than a means of getting from one place to another.

The ability to drive is liberating, exciting, sometimes intimidating. And, at least in America, learning to drive symbolizes the same coming-of-age tradition once reserved to dragging home your first kill from the hunt.

Do you remember your initial adventure behind the wheel? I don't mean the time you sat on Dad's lap while he drove into the driveway. I mean the time you turned on the key, gripped the steering wheel with sweaty hands and actually drove a car down the road.

I remember that heady, terrifying experience vividly.

I was spending the afternoon with my pal, Marty, and her family at their cottage on Lake Worth, near Ft. Worth, Texas. Marty's dad, a dear, old-fashioned country doctor, had just bought a new Studebaker.

Outside the window of the cottage, the jet black car glowed in the Texas sunshine, a pointy-nosed chariot just yearning to take to the road. And Marty, a few months older than I, had her license.

She begged her dad to let her give me a ride in the new beauty. Since he couldn't deny his baby anything, he handed her the keys, after cautioning her to take it easy.

In a moment, we were rolling along the narrow, winding dirt roads. Marty carefully guided the car as we felt the full swell of this important occasion. We were on our own!

After ten minutes or so of enjoying the power and prestige of her first solo trip in the new buggy, Marty looked over at me and asked, "Wanna try it?"

Did I! No wonder I loved this special girlfriend. It was as though she could read my mind.

She slipped out of the driver's seat and I hurriedly scooted in. For just a moment, I simply held the wheel. The power I felt was incredible.

Finally, I turned the key and shifted into low…ah, yes, this was in those early driving days of the old stick shift.

For long minutes I navigated the narrow road in that dreadful lurching, head-snapping, gut-tightening ride that only a learning driver, trying to conquer the intricacies of clutching and shifting, can accomplish. Although I finally managed to smooth the trip out a bit, we decided Marty had better take over again.

It's been over forty years since that first session behind the wheel. I've logged many miles in a wide variety of cars. There have been Buicks and Chevrolets, Pontiacs and Fords. And my all-time favorite, a little beauty of a Rambler Metropolitan. It was so small, I could sit in the driver's seat and clean all the windows.

Both cars and I have come a long way. I deeply appreciate such advancements as automatic transmissions, defrosters and air conditioning. The comfort and safety of today's vehicles has taken driving to a new level.

But, no matter what experiences you've had behind the wheel, nothing will ever quite equal the thrill of that first chance to actually operate a car.

Even today, when I see a shiny black Studebaker at one of those classic car shows, I feel the urge to slide into the driver's seat, just for old time's sake.

"Have You Seen My Wife?"

Not long ago, I saw our friend, Dick, in one of the area's giant discount stores. He greeted me distractedly as his eyes searched the crowds. Finally, he admitted, "I think I've lost my wife. Have you seen her?"

Dick's question made me realize, throughout this vast country at any given moment, there are countless lonely men wandering aimlessly through malls, grocery stores and shopping centers in search of their missing mates. It's become a national crisis.

Things were quite different in the communities of yesterday. One factor keeping couples together during such outings, was that shopping opportunities were limited. With only three or four stores on the town's block-long Main Street, it was difficult for anyone to be lost for long. If the wife ended up at the dress shop, she could be sure her husband would find her after his stop at the hardware store across the street.

Now, with malls large enough to hold the entire population of some towns, it's little wonder pairs often become singles.

Another reason the couples of old stayed together during their shopping trips was that the man carried the family funds. It was his job to pay for the purchases.

When today's wives bag up their bargains, they use that equal-opportunity payment genie, the plastic credit card. A modern wife can make a dozen purchases in the time it would once have taken to talk her hubby out of the necessary cash for just one.

The "lost wife" syndrome would be simple to solve if husbands could remember what their mate was wearing. At least they would have some visual clues to guide them in their search for their beloved. But, as most every wife realizes, once she changes from her wedding gown, what she wears in public is seldom imprinted on her husband's memory.

In order to help men who have lost their wives in the shopping scene, I've come up with two possible solutions.

First, for their trips to the mall or Wal-Mart, the couple could dress alike in eye-catching outfits. The ideal choice would be clothes with little chance of duplication by others…green tie-dyed shirts and maroon shorts, perhaps. Using this clothing-locator method, the husband would only have to reexamine his own outfit, then walk the hallways and store aisles looking for a match.

The second method could be utilized if all else fails. In this case, the couple would take along on their outing one of those nifty little bike flags that make cyclists visible in traffic. As a wife-locator, the flag would be attached to the lady's shopping cart, purse, or, in the absence of these, her head, using a head-band. This would allow the hubby to keep track of his mate's movements by noting the position of the airborne flag.

If, however, this innovative approach should catch on with shoppers, there could be a forest of flags filling shopping centers.

And there once again, wandering aimlessly through the crowds, scores of lonely husbands would be searching for their lost wives.

Math is Different in the Home

Through the years, experience has taught me that within the walls of the American home, the rules of math we all learned in school simply don't apply. Where family living is involved, the logical concepts of addition, subtraction, multiplication and division are lost in the confusion.

Take hangers, for instance.

Logic tells us that two hangers plus two hangers make four hangers. Right?

Not in my closets!

I can take a couple of things out of my section of our double closet, leaving the hangers bare. My husband does the same. Now there are four empty hangers mixed in with the clothes. Only four.

Yet somehow, when the closet doors close, strange things happen. That's when the clothes-less hangers do whatever their kind do. By the time I finally notice what's been going on, I have a dozen hangers pushing and shoving the clothes out of the way, making space for some sort of hanger reunion.

A couple of times a year, I gather up the extras and give them away...and still they keep coming.

The hanger explosion only stops on wash day. Then, no matter how hard I search, I'm lucky to come up with one useful hanger. It's as though word spreads behind the closet doors and the able-bodied hanger population finds a way to transport itself to a less dangerous closet to carry on its festivities.

Addition and subtraction as we know them don't apply to socks, either.

The problem here lies not in the closet, but in the laundry.

I can put four perfectly-matched pairs of socks into the wash. According to the logic of math, that means there are eight socks now swishing around in the suds. Yet, somehow, when the final count is taken after the team comes out of the dryer, one unfortunate member has fallen victim to the sock snatcher.

I know somewhere out there lies a huge mountain of mate-less socks, waiting to be reunited with their missing twins.

The mountain is part of the land of lost items. It's where all the new, sharpened pencils go, leaving behind only tiny stubs, barely long enough to grasp.

This land of the lost is also home to things that routinely subtract themselves from our lives…one of my favorite gold earrings, the Jack of spades which somehow left our deck of cards without warning, the spare key to the shed. They're all out there somewhere.

Then there's the way math as we know it is twisted in the kitchen.

When I was a teen-ager, countless afternoons I came home from school so hungry I could eat the shelf paper in the cabinets. The refrigerator would reveal such sparse offerings as a small chunk of cold meat loaf and a cup of tomato paste. That's when I'd complain dramatically to Mom, "There's nothing to eat and I'm starving!"

She always found an apple or orange to tide me over till supper. Then somehow the table would be filled with a huge bowl of steaming spaghetti drenched in Mom's delicious meat sauce.

I never understood how she managed to make so much from so little…until I became a mother. Now I practice the same wizardry in my own kitchen. It's amazing how a cup of this, a handful of that and a pinch of something else…with a little imagination thrown in…can make a satisfying meal for the whole family.

The magic is an undeniable part of what goes on within the walls of the home. Nothing in the math books can explain it. Yet those of us who endlessly gather extra hangers, search behind the appliances for a missing sock or whip up a meal out of nothing, realize logic doesn't apply where family life is concerned.

I've Turned Another Calendar Page

The calendar has just rolled around to another of those increasingly frequent annual observances called my birthday.

When I was a kid, the thing I most hated to hear was, "You're just going to have to wait till you get a little older." Though it seemed to me I waited and waited, the birthdays were agonizingly slow in coming.

Now I hang up a new calendar in January and, in what seems only a few weeks, it's down to the November page again. I guess it's true what that great "Snoopy" philosopher, Charles Schultz said: "Once you're over the hill, you begin to pick up speed."

Every year at this time, as I make another mental notch on the yardstick of my life, I search for words of wisdom from others who have passed this way before. The quotes generally prove that getting older doesn't necessarily mean getting wiser, but it does seem to increase your ability to laugh at life.

For instance, Robert Orbin said, "Old people shouldn't eat health foods. They need all the preservatives they can get."

Comic Joey Adams greeted the inevitable with, "Don't worry about avoiding temptation. As you grow older, it will avoid you."

But I heard one of the best quotes on aging from the slightly twisted wisdom of Rose Nyland, Betty White's delightful character on the old Golden Girls television series. She said, "My mother always used to say, 'The older you get, the better you get...unless you're a banana.'"

While reading over the observations of others, I've also been taking stock of some of the things I've learned on my own while moseyin' along on the bumpy road of life.

For example, I've decided the fashion gurus who determine what the with-it women of the world should wear, have a basic desire to humiliate their mothers. The emphasis on young, supple bodies in short skirts totally excludes my creaky, over-the-hill form with legs best kept out of sight.

And in recent years, there have been so many interesting changes in my face I now find the safest time to look into the bathroom mirror is immediately after a shower. A looking glass covered with steam makes for a much more acceptable reflection.

But on the positive side, it's wonderful to put to use all the knowledge I've gathered through the years. Most came not from college or special training, but simply from living life with eyes and ears wide open.

I've learned to accept those things I can't change, say "no" to things I really don't want to do and relish those things that bring me joy.

The latter includes experiences I always avoided during my fast-paced growing-up years. Since I've slowed down a little, I can enjoy stopping by a lake to watch a family of ducks or to study the changing cloud formations reflected in the water. And I often drive down unfamiliar roads, just to see where they lead. At this age, I take time to savor each new day.

Another blessing of this far-side-of-middle-age time of my life is the realization that most problems simply aren't worth worrying about. They are so quickly replaced by other, more interesting concerns.

While taking note of my birthday, I've looked around my world and decided I have a lot in common with our well-used kitchen table, a sturdy wooden affair that has served the family well for many years.

It's broad, comfortable and covered with scrapes and nicks from a lifetime of daily interactions with family and friends. But both the old table and I still look presentable when given a little loving care and a fresh coat of polish. Chances are we'll both be around doing our jobs for quite a while.

All in all, I'm enjoying myself more today than at any other time in my life. November is bound to get here again much faster than I expect, but I'm having too much fun to worry about the next turning of that calendar page.

A Nation of Walking Billboards

Between the seasonal sweatshirts and the novelty tee shirts, everyone you meet is spreading some message on their clothing these days. It's a new twist to an old advertising technique.

When I was a kid, my neighbor, Charlie, got a summer job wearing a sandwich-board sign. Each day he became a walking ad, marching back and forth in front of Taylor's Ice Cream Store with the sign that invited folks to stop for a treat.

All of us were jealous of Charlie's success. Not only was he getting lots of free ice cream, he was earning money while becoming a neighborhood celebrity.

Today, the messages we wear on our front and backsides fit better than Charlie's cumbersome sandwich-board. On the down side, however, we're not getting a weekly check. In fact, we pay well for the privilege of advertising some favorite product, team, celebrity or event. Message sweatshirts and tees have become a huge business.

In our neck of the woods, the Buffalo Bills account for the majority of the jackets and other team-related wearing apparel. But the Bills don't have a corner on these body billboards. Every pro football, baseball, hockey, and basketball team has thousands of folks out there displaying the team name on upper-body clothing.

Universities, too, are high on the list of tee and sweatshirt advertisers.

Then there are the hundreds of "message" shirts that find their way into wardrobes. Our son, Tim, has a rainbow of these colorful tops jamming his dresser drawers. They include tees from long-ago events like the Findley Lake Fire Department Canoe Races of 1980 and the Mayville Ice Castle Extravaganza of 1989. The collection also includes shirts commemorating everything from bowling tournaments to bicycle races.

One of Tim's favorites may eventually become a collector's item. The teeshirt was inspired by a popular ad of a few seasons ago. It reads, "Here's the beef."

The latest addition to the "message" teeshirt is a new and innovative line called The Cotton Quarterly. These shirts, designed by an enterprising west coast writer, contain an entire short story...T-shorts, he calls them. The developer claims that everywhere he goes, people pause to read him from front to back. It's a unique concept and will certainly be a welcome relief from those shirts that say such clever things as "If you can read this, you're too close," or the one with the downward arrow worn by moms-in-waiting telling the world she has a "Baby on board."

With the variety of messages and designs available on sweats and tees, it's no wonder these wearable signs and displays have become so popular. They certainly beat Charlie's old sandwich-board sign. Unfortunately, today's comfortable body billboards don't come with the bonus of that delicious Taylor's ice cream.

Love By the Bowlful

A popular slogan boasts, "nothin' says lovin' like something from the oven." But, for me, loving is conjured up in a big kettle of homemade soup.

During my childhood years, I recall Mom would often work her special kitchen magic by concocting in a single pot the most magnificent meal of all, vegetable soup.

I didn't realize it until I became an adult, but the frequent use of soup in our diet was Mom's way of stretching our food budget during some tough financial times. As a kid, I simply found the contents of those slow-simmering kettles delicious.

When I became a bride, I begged Mom for the recipe to her special one-pot wonder. She looked surprised and said with a laugh, "But there's no recipe. You just use whatever you have."

Apparently, whatever I've had in my kitchen has never matched what Mom worked with. No matter what combination of ingredients I've tried, I've never been able to duplicate that matchless taste. But, year after year, I keep trying.

One of the amazing characteristics of homemade soup is the mellowing of its flavor. As delicious as it is on that first, steeped-to-perfection day, most soups actually improve by day number two. I've seldom had the chance to try a bowl on day number three. In our family, homemade soup simply doesn't hang around that long.

In addition to being a certifiable feast in its own right, homemade soup is often praised for its healing properties.

We've all heard of the positive effects of home-cooked chicken soup. Well, believe it or not, in the interest of protecting the nation's health, the Food and Drug Administration actually did a study on the subject some twenty-five years ago. (Our tax dollars at work again!) The published results showed chicken soup is as good as any over-the-counter cold medication.

Even the prestigious Mount Sinai Medical Center looked into the subject. Researchers there confirmed that chicken soup, eaten warm, helps to break up congestion. In addition, it supplies nutrients and fluids.

And the pampered feeling that comes when someone offers a mug of homemade chicken soup also helps the sniffle-sufferer to feel better.

I don't know about official government findings, congestion relief, or the relative merits of nutrients and fluids. I only know that for me and my family, when it comes to lovin' from the kitchen, nothing beats a bowlful of homemade soup.

Things I'd Rather Not Know

Since childhood, curiosity has kept me asking questions, looking for answers, sometimes making a real pest of myself. But, as the years passed and I reached the age of AARP, I discovered there are many things I'd just as soon not know about.

For instance, I'm not interested in learning what they put into hot dogs or frozen chicken patties.

I'd rather be kept in the dark about the preservatives they have to add to those little pre-packaged cups of pudding to give them a shelf life of two years.

Don't bother telling me that gourmets swear rattlesnake meat tastes just like chicken. It's enough for me that chicken tastes like chicken.

In the area of politics, I find I have no interest in the plans Gary Condit has made for the future...although I'll bet they include a book deal and, possibly, a TV movie-of-the-week.

Bill Clinton can keep his intentions for his Harlem office to himself. I wouldn't take the time to read a magazine spread that included the proposed lay-out, the cost of furnishings and a grouping of photos showing Clinton's "magnificent sweeping view."

The media can pass me by with such information as which baseball players are getting the highest paychecks for the coming season or the football "heroes" who are now on the list of the country's newest millionaires.

Come to think of it, Donald Trump's activities are beyond my caring, too. "The Donald" seems to be one of those self-absorbed fellows who swagger down the road of life holding their own hand. He certainly doesn't need my attention.

On the topic of natural wonders, please don't give me a scientific explanation of why the maple trees are once again displaying the glory of their fall finery. It's enough for me that Mother Nature continues to make each autumn a magnificent celebration.

Forgive me if I'm not interested in the list of "named hurricanes" projected for the 2002 season. The folks who spend their time studying weather patterns on their crystal ball computers are, I'm sure, only trying to help us simple folk prepare for what they think maybe…might possibly…could perhaps lie ahead.

In the world of fad/fashion, I'm not at all curious about which body part will be the next targeted for piercing by the "in" crowd.

And I really don't care about the latest fashion trend to be unveiled by Brittany Spears in her search to be the "navel" queen of the music scene.

As far as the world of technology is concerned, the folks at Microsoft needn't bother trying to explain to me how the e-mail messages I send out can reach their target in an instant. I do, however, understand what happens when I put a stamp on a letter and drop it in one of those big blue boxes.

As time goes by, the list of things I don't care to know gets longer and longer. I've decided it boils down to this: in our complex, technological, trend loving, modern world, ignorance really is bliss.

Hey, That Looks Like...

I think it was Ogden Nash who observed that middle age is the time of life when everyone you meet looks like someone you already know.

If that's an indication of middle age, I've definitely reached the milestone. Everywhere I turn, I see familiar faces.

Yesterday, as I went into a store, I noticed a gentleman sitting on a bench outside, having a cup of coffee. I was convinced it was Ray, the husband of my Mayville friend, Mary. But, when he turned his head, I realized, as I always do, I had made a mistake.

Although this dilemma seems to affect many of us in the over-the-hill category, it's especially common for the snowbird set. With well established groups of friends in both the north and south, opportunities for confusion are doubled.

Fortunately, my usual companion for grocery shopping, both here in Punta Gorda and back home in Mayville, is son Tim. He is much less likely to fall victim to the problem of misplaced identity than I.

Last week's shopping trip was a good example. As I cruised the aisles, I spotted a familiar figure just rounding the corner ahead. I sped up a bit to get a better look at the lady. I was sure my Mayville pal, Pat, had somehow made it down to Florida. Over my shoulder to Tim I repeated the question I seem to be asking more frequently these days. "Isn't that...?"

Before I could finish, Tim said in a here-we-go-again voice, "Trust me, Mom, it's not."

And, when the lady stopped to take a can from the shelf, I realized he was right. The walk was the same. The hair style was the same. But the face was that of a stranger.

It's not just a glimpse of a person that can stop me in mid stride. Sometimes, especially in a crowd, I will hear a voice nearby that sounds exactly like the voice of a far-away chum. I turn, fully expecting to see that familiar face only to find someone else.

If Ogden Nash was right and this problem of misplaced identities is a sign of middle age, it's bound to get worse as the years go by. After all, we each gather more friends and acquaintances along the way.

Seeing these folks even when they're not there, seems to be part of the process. At one time or another, we will all catch a glimpse of someone and say to ourselves, "Wait a minute! Isn't that…"

As a veteran of frequent identity confusion, take my word for it. Chances are, it isn't.

Crystal Balls Aren't for Me

When the new millennium opened, it set us all to wondering what lies ahead. Experts from every field of endeavor made bold predictions about the days, months and years ahead. Fortunately, none of us really knows for sure just what's in store.

I recall that in my long-ago childhood years, I had a favorite fantasy. I dreamed that one day I would able to see into the future. A second dream was the ability to become invisible.

Although I still think invisibility would be a useful skill in certain situations, I'm very grateful I was never cursed with the capacity to predict what's ahead. It might be interesting to foresee the good things ahead on life's pathway, but learning about the bad news in store down the road could simply double the worry, compound the sorrow.

One of my favorite quotes came from the author of *Out of Africa*. The writer wisely observed, "The earth was made round so that we would not see too far down the road."

Maturity has shown me the wisdom of that thought. I enjoy dreaming about what's in store, but knowing is another thing entirely.

My Mom occasionally surprised the family with her uncanny knack for looking into the future. The talent seemed to be a combination of a mother's intuition and good-guessmanship. It gave her a reputation as a chronic worrier. She even admitted she often "borrowed trouble" from tomorrow.

From time to time, I've read stories of those reportedly "blessed" with premonitions of events yet to come. In every case, the ability caused pain and anxiety.

Some folks are convinced astrology holds the key to knowing the future in advance. Like most people, I sometimes look over the astrology columns in the papers, checking out what the star-guided analyzers say is in store for me.

If astrology is your bag, I apologize for my skepticism. But, I've always found these Zodiac based peeks at the future are so general they could fit anyone. The self-proclaimed experts can hardly go wrong with such non-specific predictions as, "You may experience financial problems" or "Stress at home."

I'm not disappointed that my future isn't spelled out in the horoscope columns, nor in the alignment of the stars. I don't really want to know what tomorrow, next week or next year will bring.

Just think what the ability to foretell the future might reveal. You could know in advance if your stock was going to rise or if the lottery jackpot would be yours. On the other hand, you might learn that you would lose your job or your health.

You could foresee a relaxing trip to Hawaii. But you could also find out just when your dog or cat would die.

No, a crystal ball is one of those childhood dreams I'm glad was never fulfilled.

But, I'll admit, I'd still like to give that invisibility thing a try.

Memories of a Make Believe Christmas Village

Early each December during my childhood years, the everyday knick-knacks on the fireplace mantel were replaced by a traditional tribute to the season, the family's Christmas village.

As the youngest of four, my sister Lynn and I were the designated village builders. It was a shared effort that gave us not only a favorite holiday decoration, but lasting Christmas memories.

Buildings and people for our little community were borrowed from our older brothers' model railroad set. The collection included a few tiny houses, a long train station and a lovely white church with a steeple pointing heavenward.

Each of the miniature buildings had glassine windows looking out on the world. The panes in the church were of varied colors, simulating stained glass. And, in the back wall of each structure, there was a round opening designed to accept a bulb from a string of Christmas lights. The illumination shone through the windows, making the whole scene glow from the mantel when daylignt faded on those long evenings during the holiday season.

Like patient giants, Lynn and I moved the buildings around until we were satisfied with the arrangement. Somehow, the church always became the centerpiece.

The next step was to install lights. It was an annual challenge to chose exactly the right color for each building.

Should the train station be lit with yellow? How about a heavenly blue for the church? And, would a soft green suit the little cottage on the corner?

Once the lights were set, it was time to bring on the snow. Mom donated flour and the sifter for the project, then left us to our creativity. Lynn and I were in charge of snow production and clean-up. With sisterly enthusiasm, we always accomplished the task, though there was a fair amount of fall-out on the living room carpet.

People were the final addition to our fireplace community. Although these little plaster figures were designed to stand by the railroad station and out buildings on the model train lay-out, Lynn and I were convinced they looked forward to their Christmas vacation in our charming village.

One of my favorites was an elegant lady in a dark coat, hat and gloves. She held the mittened hand of a small boy, who walked by her side. We usually placed the pair in front of one of the cottages.

The train conductor, with the gold watch chain across his mid-section, was on duty at the train station.

The village residents also included a young man holding a lantern above his head. His position on the model railroad lay-out was beside one of the train switches. But, here in the village, he stood at the end of the street, as if lighting the way for his neighbors.

The last resident, a distinguished gentleman with a top hat and grey coat, was placed near the church.

When Lynn and I finished the project, we darkened the living room and turned on the village lights. Our first look at the tiny, snow-covered community, glowing with the beauty of Christmas, was always the highlight of our early holiday preparations.

Though it has long been gone, that little village still glows with warmth and wonder in my memory.

It continues to remind me of the villages, towns and big cities around the world that, even today, are basking in the light of the Christmas season. From Mayville to Madrid, from Sherman to Sydney, from Westfield to Warsaw, commuities are prepared once again to mark the miracle that came to all of us so long ago in the form of the Chirst Child.

The Christmas of
Big Brown Bear

During the Christmas season, nostalgia seems to run high for all of us. Like Dickens' Scrooge and his dream time visitors, we go back to Christmases past, and the memories are ever green.

This week, while going over my list of gifts yet to find, I lapsed into a reverie about the Christmas gifts I have received throughout the years. Although I have been most grateful for the wonderful presents that have come my way, there is one gift that stands out as the best of the bunch. It was from my brother.

As the youngest of four, I had two older brothers and a sister. Bob, who was 15 years older than I, lived away from home. He wasn't a part of my childhood world.

My personal hero was my second brother, Alan. Since he was ten years older, he seemed to be the personification of all the things I wanted to be: smart, popular and, best of all, grown up.

I suppose when I was five and Alan was 15, this admiration was only in its formative stage. But by the time I was 10 and he was 20, I had a full-blown case of hero worship. What made my love for this larger-than-life person so poignant was that Alan was far away, attending college in North Dakota.

Now, if you live in South Dakota, Minnesota, or even Montana, North Dakota isn't so far away. When you're a ten-year-old, living in Texas, North Dakota might as well be next-door to Mars. I was convinced I had lost my brother/hero for good.

When Christmas rolled around that year, I had a hard time finding the customary joy in the season. Even the traditional excitement of decorating the house, crafting presents for loved ones and joining my sister, Lynn, for our usual fruitless search for hidden presents didn't lift my spirits. There was a giant hole in my world where my brother should have been.

Then, just when it seemed my tenth Christmas would be a wash-out, a huge box arrived from North Dakota. Inside were packages for the whole family. Alan had remembered everyone. And for me, he had included the largest and fanciest box of all.

That year the sweet suspense of waiting for Christmas morning was almost unbearable. But finally the great day dawned…somewhere around 5 a.m., as I recall.

The first present I tore into was, of course, Alan's beautiful box. I had been opening it in fantasy since the day it came.

Inside, under all the wrapping and tissue, there was the special gift that became so much more than just a Christmas present.

It was a teddy bear unlike any I had ever seen. Not one of those little wimpy, ribbons-and-bows toys that simply sit on a shelf, this was a substantial kind of bear, one to lose your heart to. It was the perfect companion, designed to survive the rigors of life as a tomboy's side-kick.

The bear was two-feet tall and sturdy, yet cuddly. The short, soft brown fur on his plump body was complimented by the deep brown of his paws. Above all was the wise gaze of his shoe-button eyes. They seemed to understand that his role in life was to be the best friend of a little girl who didn't really believe in stuffed toys. No wonder I fell hopelessly in love with this special gift.

From that first day, this priceless present from the heart of my loving big brother, became my best pal. I named him simply ``Big Brown Bear''.

As the years went by, he was showered with hugs and kisses, was dressed in countless costumes, and was a participant in every part of my life. He rode in the basket of my bike, attended meetings of my childhood clubs, and waited on my bed while I was at school.

When those wonderful/terrible teen years came along, my best friend dried many a tear of frustration, heart-break and anger on his fuzzy brown body.

Then, as I entered my college years, Big Brown Bear became a constant part of the background of my life. With his shiny shoe-button eyes, he stood watch as I rushed off to class and sat quietly through many a late-night session of cramming for exams.

For a short time after I got married, Big Brown Bear was tucked away for a well deserved period of hibernation. Then, when I became a mother, Big Brown Bear was lovingly released from his packing to serve the honored role of companion to a new generation of little ones. Once again there were wagon rides and afternoon naps, hugs and dress-up sessions.

Through the years, his dark-chocolate paws were patched and he lost one of his shiny shoe-button eyes to a childhood tug-of-war. But he was soon outfitted with a new pair of buttons eyes in a soft shade of brown. They gave him the more mature look of an elder statesman who had seen much and understood it all.

Now a fully qualified adult in his own right, Big Brown Bear has found his permanent home with our oldest daughter, Becky. He is serving as a trusted companion for granddaughter Rachel. When we visited recently, there in Rachel's bright and sunny room sat my old pal.

As he and I shared a hug, all the memories came flooding back.

I'm sure he knew that inside this grown up lady, there was still the same little girl who looked in wonder into the box on that long-ago Christmas morning. And for my part, I saw past the soft brown button eyes to the shiny shoe buttons that captured my heart from that first moment.

The Ghost of Christmas Yet to Come

Unlike old Ebenezer Scrooge, I welcome my seasonal visit from the Ghost of Christmas Past. He brings priceless memories of family gatherings through the years.

And the Ghost of Christmas Present lets me glimpse the joy of this year's celebration of Christ's birth.

But the Ghost of Christmas Yet to Come is a sorrowful visitor. The future Christmas scenes he has shown me are far different from those of my childhood...or the childhood of my own children.

This spirit of what lies ahead tells me that one day, small children will know Christmas only as a time of Santa Claus, candy, glowing lights and fancy packages. The day will come when somewhere, amid the tinsel and trappings of another yuletide, a little boy will notice an antique ornament of an angel. If he asks his parents the story of the small haloed cherub, will they remember?

And across the land, in government buildings and public places, halls will be decked with holly and mistletoe. Yet in no park, no village square, no town hall, no Washington chamber will there be a softly lighted scene of a young mother tenderly holding her newborn son as a reverent Joseph stands quietly by and lowly shepherds kneel in worship.

In schools throughout the country the songs of the season will focus on snow and jingle bells, sleigh rides and Santa Claus (as long as he isn't referred to SAINT Nicholas). Children who are never taken to church will not learn to sing "Away in a Manger" or "Silent Night" or

"O Little Town of Bethlehem." If, on some far off December evening, a little girl asks her mommy to teach her some of the "old" Christmas songs, will her mother recall them?

The Ghost of Christmas Yet to Come shows a future of even more Christmastide stress as people lose the season's joy and peace in their rush to out-spend, out-give, and out-do each other.

And, in the future, the word may be permanently shortened from Christmas to Xmas. The change will not only streamline our writing but will remove the name that some feel is unnecessary for the celebration of the season.

The Ghost of Christmas Yet to Come fears that in Christmas seasons of the future, the miracle of Jesus' birth may only be told in the churches. Here, those who have heard the story will gather to hear it once again, to share the message of the coming of the Messiah.

But what of the weary world so in need of the story of hope, joy, and peace? What of those who don't visit the churches? Where will the children and their busier-than-ever parents hear those words that radiate like the light of the star, the light that has shown down through the generations? Where will they learn of the Christ of Christ-mas?

The Ghost of Christmas Yet to Come looks ahead and, sometimes, he cries.

Some Assembly Required

During the recent holiday shopping season, I noticed more items than ever with labels warning "some assembly required".

Bicycles and book cases, computer desks and bunk beds...all depended on an investment of time and effort to transform them from a collection of random parts in a box into something useful.

Standing here at the doorway of a promising new year, I realize the collection of unspoiled new days stretching ahead of us should also carry that same some-assembly-required warning.

The folks who walk through the doorway with a well-equipped toolbox are the ones who will be most successful in crafting the best possible new year.

But what tools do we need for this challenging job?

One of the most important will be enthusiasm. Enthusiasm adds an extra sparkle to each day of life.

Curiosity is another primary tool to use in assembling a rewarding year. Question askers find the kinds of answers along the way that open up new paths, new opportunities.

As fascinating as our world has become, there are folks I've met who seem to have no interest in expanding their knowledge beyond the absolute necessities. Yet those with an insatiable thirst for knowledge constantly find new facets to this jewel called life. If we stretch our minds with curiosity, by this time next year we'll know more about ourselves, our fellow men and women and our world. It's a great way to get more out of life in the months that lie ahead.

A third vital tool for the adventures that await us starting January first is a sense of humor. There seems to be no end of sorrow and conflict out there. But if we keep our laugh lines open, we'll find enough to smile about to smooth out the inevitable pot holes in the new year's section of our road of life.

But the most important tool we can bring along to help us in building this new year is faith.

One of my favorite short prayers is, "Dear God, please help me to remember that nothing can happen to me today that You and I can't handle."

With a deep belief in God and the inborn goodness of mankind, we can face anything. Although headlines scream their incessant tales of war and wantonness, for every story that has made our blood run cold in recent months, there have been dozens of reports of bravery and self-lessness that have made us proud of our fellow humans. Unfortunately, the good stuff usually doesn't get much press. It seldom sells papers, finds its way to the talk shows, or makes the top of the evening news. But we all know folks who are shining examples of what is good and decent.

Faith in God and in our fellow man can cut through the darkest night, pull us out of the deepest hole.

Enthusiasm, curiosity, humor and faith…they are just a few of the key tools that can help us craft the collection of days ahead into a year worth remembering.

So sharpen your tools and keep them ready. Somewhere hidden away in the small print on that first calendar page of the new year will be the familiar warning, "some assembly required".

0-595-23356-2